DEMOCRACY
BETRAYED

DEMOCRACY BETRAYED

How Superdelegates, Redistricting,
Party Insiders, and the Electoral College
Rigged the 2016 Election

STEVEN ROSENFELD

Hot Books

Hot Books may be purchased in bulk at special discounts for sales promotion, corporate gifts, fund-raising, or educational purposes. Special editions can also be created to specifications. For details, contact the Special Sales Department, Skyhorse Publishing, 307 West 36th Street, 11th Floor, New York, NY 10018 or info@skyhorsepublishing.com.

Hot Books® and Skyhorse Publishing® are registered trademarks of Skyhorse Publishing, Inc.®, a Delaware corporation.

Visit our website at www.hotbookspress.com

10 9 8 7 6 5 4 3 2 1

Library of Congress Cataloging-in-Publication Data is available on file.

Cover design by Brian Peterson

Print ISBN: 978-1-5107-2945-2
Ebook ISBN: 978-1-5107-2946-9

Printed in the United States of America

I am trying to write history while it is happening
and I don't want to be wrong.

—John Steinbeck

CONTENTS

SECTION III:
The Recounts

FOREWORD
BY DAVID TALBOT

THE WORLD IS BURNING, AND YET the firelight illuminates the way out. The times are dire, even catastrophic. Nonetheless we can sense a grand awakening, a growing realization all around the globe that "people have the power, to dream, to rule, to wrestle the world from fools" in the prophetic words of Patti Smith.

But in order to rouse ourselves from the nightmares that hold us in their grip, we need to know more about the forces that bedevil us, the structures of power that profit from humanity's exploitation and from that of the earth. That's the impetus behind Hot Books, a series that seeks to expose the dark operations of power and to light the way forward.

Skyhorse publisher Tony Lyons and I started Hot Books in 2015 because we believe that books can make a difference. Since then the Hot Books series has shined a light on the cruel reign of racism and police violence in Baltimore (D. Watkins' *The Beast Side*); the poisoning of U.S. soldiers by their own environmentally reckless commanding officers (Joseph Hickman's *The Burn Pits*); the urgent need to hold U.S. officials accountable for their criminal actions during the war on terror (Rachel Gordon's *American Nuremberg*); the covert manipulation of the media by intelligence agencies (Nicholas Schou's *Spooked*); the rise of a rape culture on campus (Kirby Dick and Amy

Ziering's *The Hunting Ground*); the insidious demonizing of Muslims in the media and Washington (Arsalan Iftikhar's *Scapegoats*); the crackdown on whistleblowers who know the government's dirty secrets (Mark Hertsgaard's *Bravehearts*); the disastrous policies of the liberal elite that led to the triumph of Trump (Chris Hedges' *Unspeakable*); the American wastelands that gave rise to this dark reign (Alexander Zaitchik's *The Gilded Rage*); the energy titans and their political servants who are threatening human survival (Dick Russell's *Horsemen of the Apocalypse*); the utilization of authoritarian tactics by Donald Trump that threaten to erode American democracy (Brian Klaas's *The Despot's Apprentice*); the capture, torture, and detention of the first "high-value target" captured by the CIA after 9/11 (Joseph Hickman and John Kiriakou's *The Convenient Terrorist*); and the deportation of American veterans (J Malcolm Garcia's *Without a Country*). And the series continues, going where few publishers dare.

Hot Books are more condensed than standard-length books. They're packed with provocative information and points of view that mainstream publishers usually shy from. Hot Books are meant not just to stir readers' thinking, but to stir trouble.

Hot Books authors follow the blazing path of such legendary muckrakers and troublemakers as Upton Sinclair, Lincoln Steffens, Rachel Carson, Jane Jacobs, Jessica Mitford, I.F. Stone and Seymour Hersh. The magazines and newspapers that once provided a forum for this deep and dangerous journalism have shrunk in number and available resources. Hot Books aims to fill this crucial gap.

American journalism has become increasingly digitized and commodified. If the news isn't fake, it's usually shallow. But there's a growing hunger for information that is both credible and undiluted by corporate filters.

A publishing series with this intensity cannot keep burning in a vacuum. Hot Books needs a culture of equally passionate readers. Please spread the word about these titles—encourage your bookstores to carry them, post comments about them in online stores and forums, persuade your book clubs, schools, political groups and community organizations to read them and invite the authors to speak.

It's time to go beyond packaged news and propaganda. It's time for Hot Books . . . journalism without borders.

INTRODUCTION

IT'S MID-DECEMBER 2016 IN NEW YORK City. The sting of the presidential election has not worn off. There's a harsh wind blowing as I'm cutting across Lincoln Center for a meeting I am drawn to, but also wary about. I have been a national political reporter since the 1990s at various outlets, some mainstream like NPR and others in progressive media. Over the years, I've covered elections deeply. This is not just candidates and speeches, but who can vote, who can't, how that happens, and whether the count can be trusted. I've been pulled back into the vortex of our elections where, despite efforts to expand the vote and improve our system, the more ruthless and smarter forces have won again. You and I—and the vast majority of our fellow citizens—are the losers.

I've been here before. In 2004, I spent weeks, then months, then two years with others tracing and writing about what happened in Ohio where Republican President George W. Bush beat Democrat John Kerry. We produced a catalog of dirty tricks that Republicans have resurrected with predictable uniformity ever since. Donald Trump's surprise victories and the US Senate staying in Republican hands felt eerily familiar. Many explanations in the aftermath did not add up. In 2004, we were told a wave of rural, white southern Ohio evangelicals had reelected Bush. We looked but didn't find them. Now a different white flock—economically struggling and lacking higher education, we were told—elected Trump.[1] And the election was not even entirely over.

I was to meet Lulu Friesdat, a filmmaker who had been taking time off from her job as a CBS-TV producer to film the 2016 presidential recount in Wisconsin. We had talked on the phone about what she saw and shot. These were breakdowns where no one in an official role could verify to the satisfaction of observers and computer scientists what constituted the actual final count. Lulu witnessed it, filmed it, and was mortified. I posted her clips on AlterNet.org. She already concluded that the Democratic Party had kept the nomination from Bernie Sanders. I agreed, though we differed on particulars of its antidemocratic culture and playbook. Now Friesdat was discovering another facet of the way elections really work in America.

Her most memorable clip showed a process filled with earnest citizens; banal officials; and maddening, unnecessary complications rooted in arcane election rules. Friesdat had gone to the Racine County government center, not far from Lake Michigan. Outside the center, people were rooting for the Green Bay Packers or shopping for Christmas—but inside, the center was a world apart. Most people thought the election was over. They turned away from states certifying results, the Electoral College convention, and then Congress ratifying that vote. Interrupting this progression was the Green Party's feisty candidate, Jill Stein, who had a legal right to file for recounts in the last three states—Wisconsin, Michigan, and Pennsylvania—giving Trump his apparent victory.

Stein supporters unexpectedly had donated millions over the Thanksgiving holiday, after her legal team could not convince Hillary Clinton's campaign to enlist some of their donors. That grassroots response was completely unexpected. Like much of America, Stein's donors questioned 2016's official results. They were part of 2016's grassroots surge seeking real change, especially millennial youths. They wanted to know what happened. I'd seen the Greens file for a recount in 2004 in Ohio. That effort did not change its outcome. But it did help expose a spectrum of tactics in the fine print of voting that confirmed the GOP was committed to strategically targeting and suppressing known Democratic Party blocs. In other words, the voting process had been turned against its rightful participants.

Inside the government center, which could be any election office in America, the slow methodical business of recounting an election churned. A team of middle-aged women in sweaters parsed and fed paper ballots one-by-one into an electronic scanner. Three Green Party observers, led by Liz Whitlock from nearby Mount Pleasant, stood back and patiently watched. These Greens were well-groomed citizens in their middle years, anything but wild Bernie bros from the spring campaign. They wanted Racine County to hand count its paper ballots, citing academics that said electronic scanners like those in use have implicit error rates from misreading ink marks.

They wanted to know if Trump had really won, by how much, where his voters were, or what wasn't accurate in the process. But Joan Rennert, a veteran local official overseeing that day's recount, was losing patience in a plodding exercise where the final outcome was unlikely to change. Across the state in liberal Madison, a judge gave each Wisconsin county the option of doing a hand recount or not. Racine declined.

So Whitlock and her colleagues devised a simple work-around. They bought manual counters, mechanical hand clickers. They clicked away as each ballot slipped into the electronic scanner, tallying how many votes were for Clinton, Trump or blank—a so-called under-vote. They kept noticing their totals varied from the scanners. When Whitlock's team saw the scanner miscount fifteen votes in a three hundred–voter precinct in Elmwood Park, she politely asked officials to do a hand count of that precinct. That was an error rate of 5 percent in a contest, where statewide, Trump's margin of victory was less than 1 percent. Whitlock's request was swiftly denied.

The Greens huddled. They were upset. Whitlock then filed a challenge, a paper document that stopped the process. A face-off ensued with Rennert taking charge. Her bevy of women watched and waited, arms folded across chests, hands on their hips. Whitlock's team bowed their heads but stayed firm. It looked like a standoff between teachers and the principal's office. All appeared well-meaning. But it spiraled downhill as Friesdat's camera kept rolling.[2]

"Three observers click counted votes. The Clinton and Trump counters clicked considerable more votes than a scanner counted," said Rennert, wearily reading aloud the challenge. "I have no idea what you're saying except you are requesting a hand count."

Rennert put down the paper. She looked at the room, palms up, exasperated. She said nothing.

"Do you want to ask me if you don't understand?" asked Whitlock.

"No," Rennert tartly replied. "Is this the purpose of a hand count? Yes or No?"

"The purpose of a hand count is to get to the truth," Whitlock replied.

"No," Rennert said, her hands up like stop signs. "How much is it?"

"Three-hundred," a worker said, referring to the number of ballots.

"I don't care if it's five," Rennert declared. "I am not going to do a hand count for anybody."

I don't have to tell you who had the final word. Nor whether the official vote count matched the hand clickers or computer scanners. Stubbornness and institutional inertia won.

This small scene points to one of the great ironies of our time. Our system of voting has increasingly subverted American democracy. How that has happened, how it was seen in 2016 and its precursors this decade, and why that matters is the subject of this book. The antidemocratic features in our elections are betraying the country, its citizens, and our collective future. This is a bigger problem than which party or factions win or lose—although those most responsible for this crisis, the Republicans, have triumphed.

The scene in Racine's government center was a microcosm of the fragility, imperfections, opaqueness, and frustrations that all too often comprises American elections. The volunteers and workers weren't bent on bad will, but they weren't to up to the job, given its seriousness and its stakes. Their ineptitude and stonewalling were less excusable because these weren't overwhelmed poll workers, but arms of local government that should have known and done better.

Notably, this snapshot didn't even involve hard-core political types—the partisans, in our era almost exclusively Republicans, who deliberately undermine their opponents' base at many key steps along the way before the vote count. I had been in Friesdat's shoes, discovering slights that undermined the public's expectation that every vote mattered, every voter was equal and all ballots would be counted. When I went to meet her, the unofficial results—another GOP sweep—were raw. I had not delved into the minutiae of elections for several years. I wasn't a newcomer, but 2016 was different—and not just Trump's ugly path.

After reporting on Ohio, I covered the 2008 election as a voting rights beat and saw how President Obama's landslide breached the anti-voter barriers we documented. These were micro-aggressions that would have favored Republicans in a closer race had the economy not crashed that fall. These attacks are embedded in the fine-print rules of voting. They are almost always presented by politicians and regulators as neutral changes or safeguards or colorblind. In reality they shape who votes and is likely to win. They favor a status quo that is almost always the GOP's shrinking, aging, largely white, and suburban base.

For example, restricting the forms of state-issued ID required to get a ballot at a polling place. Or adding an extra requirement on a state voter registration form that's not on the federal form, found in every post office. Those moves block students, people of color, and the poor, just as they are intended to do. Or curtailing early voting on the weekend before Election Day, when clergy urge congregations to go to the polls. Or rejecting ballots turned in at the wrong table in a polling place. Or darker tactics such as top state officials knowingly using error-prone databases to purge infrequent voters, but not telling anyone until they show up to vote. Or deliberately segregating Democratic voters into a smaller number of urban districts and spreading out those in suburbs and rural areas when drawing political maps so that the Democrats will never win.

In 2009, I joined a team at the Pew Center on the States to modernize voter registration. After Obama's blue wave, I felt improving turnout was the key to changing our politics. Pew's ensuing data center included identifying all the eligible voters in a state and then contacting them and urging them to register. By 2016, it was used by twenty states and helped break a national record for registered voters. But most of these new voters were not in the swing states. Something else was going on in states that determined who controlled the US House, that kept turning purple states red and was pivotal in electing the president. As I was drawn into covering 2016's recounts, I was jarred by a series of deepening reminders that whatever progress had been made was being overshadowed where it mattered the most.

I knew what Friesdat thought in Racine. This was not the democracy we expect, not when citizens cannot verify the count. She was doing math in her head—just like we did in Ohio. If the voting machine error she saw was anything close to routine in a state with 2,976,150 presidential votes, it could mean up to 150,000 ballots were incorrectly tallied. That might negate Trump's 22,000-vote victory. It might not. The only way to find out was not widely happening—observable hand counts. Of course, it is easy to say this is reading too much into one incident. But I, too, kept seeing a system not defaulting on behalf of voters—America's citizens.

My moment of outrage came a few days before. In Michigan's capital, Chris Thomas, the white-haired, taciturn, veteran state election director was lecturing reporters about his state's recount that had just begun. Thomas has survived decades of working for Democrats and Republicans. This includes Republicans that glibly say that hordes of phantom Democratic voters are stealing elections and not getting caught, which is a knowing lie. I'd met him in Pew's effort and thought he was shrewd enough to avoid partisan ploys. I was wrong.

Thomas cultivated a hardheaded persona. But he had also finessed an impressive work-around for people who, at the last minute, show up at polling places and aren't on voter lists. High-stakes races always have people like that. They are eligible voters but never update their registration or bother to register. During 2016's caucuses and primaries, Democratic Party rules and administrative barriers blocked these enthusiasts from voting. That hurt Bernie Sanders in several key states. New York was the worst, where its rules blocked anyone from voting in April's primary that had not registered with a party six months earlier. Thomas devised a slick way to allow these impulsive people to vote while cutting red tape. Instead of giving them a provisional ballot—which isn't counted right away because it has to be verified, he created a form with an oath. They would swear they were state residents, US citizens, eligible voters, and would vote via a regular ballot. That is unadvertised Election Day registration—a pro-voter move that Republicans have shut down in many red states.

But now, in December 2016, Thomas was on Michigan TV stating nearly 60 percent of Detroit's ballots could not be recounted. The reason given was because poll workers had mislabeled the boxes the paper ballots were put in while cleaning up on Election night. Or the numbers of ballots listed outside the boxes didn't match the ballots inside. Most were off by a few, often less than ten. Or seals on storage boxes did not look perfectly tight. Or the boxes were banged up. To the GOP, this apparent sloppiness was turned into accusations of ballot tampering by Democrats. Imaginary threats to the integrity of the process are what Republicans love to cite and hype—especially if it helps them win. They never put voters first and abide by the results. More than half of Detroit's presidential ballots were deemed ineligible for the recount. Votes that might have tipped the state were taken off the table.

That conclusion was just what Thomas' political bosses wanted. Michigan Republicans, led by the state Attorney General Bill

Schuette, joined Trump's campaign to block a recount. They ignored Trump's rants that the voting was error prone and not-to-be-trusted until he won. They declared there was no reason to recount the state. Such double standards are predictable in this fold. They shrugged at the fact that Michigan had Trump's closest margin nationwide: just eleven thousand votes out of 4.8 million ballots cast. Some seventy-five thousand ballots did not show a vote for president, Michigan's secretary of state office reported on its website.

That last omission is always suspicious. That's because people tend to vote for the high-profile races if they vote at all. Maybe some of these seventy-five thousand ballots had presidential votes, but they were not properly scanned. If a good number were from around Detroit, which went two-to-one for Clinton, maybe Trump did not win Michigan after all. Local election activists pointed to a 1950s state law that gave discretion to election officials to examine and recount every paper ballot. But Thomas went on TV saying it would not be done. Detroit's election director followed his cue, apologizing for the sorry state of voting in his city.

Knowing someone who could have quickly solved one of 2016's answerable questions rattled me. Thomas and Detroit officials could have sided with that black majority city's voters. Instead, this incident was a brazen reminder of the GOP ethic that one can never over-police the process or do too much to twist the rules in pursuit of victory. Michigan's GOP didn't care if a display of apparent institutional racism and voter suppression were a means to that end. Not surprisingly, they stopped the recount in court days later—much as the Supreme Court had infamously shut down Florida's recount in 2000, making George W. Bush president.

Following the recount was mesmerizing and jarring. It wasn't doing what a democratic process is supposed to do—provide assurances that the result is accurate. Instead, it was exposing a starker and more cynical side of elections. The answer to Michigan's seventy-five thousand under-votes was not computer science. It was examining the vote: looking at individual ballots to see if a vote was there or not. That is straightforward. That was not the same as bringing in cyber detectives to hunt for code-altering fingerprints in voting software to see if the count is being tweaked to one side's benefit. That's what the Greens wanted to do in Michigan, Wisconsin, and Pennsylvania. But that wasn't to be, either.

I'd also forgotten how rickety the country's voting machines are. Most are run on operating systems from the early 2000s—before the first iPhones. The software is proprietary, i.e. trade secrets. That is a consequence of Congress' dumb decision to support a privatized voting machine industry after Florida's mess. The election transparency watchdogs I knew were more worried about overly eager Republicans or libertarians with hacking skills than the Russians, despite intelligence agencies saying Russia infiltrated the Democratic Party and several statewide voter registration databases. Officials from Obama to FBI Director James Comey said the vote-counting process was secure. They said the machinery was so old-tech, so decentralized, and not even connected to the Internet that it couldn't be gamed to flip statewide results, or, in turn, seize the presidency.

Those reassurances buckled near Milwaukee. John Brakey, an Arizona voting transparency activist who knows more about the electronic vulnerabilities of voting machines than most local election officials, had gone to Wisconsin to observe the Greens' recount. He spotted a hacking pathway into the vote count tabulators. I am not by nature a conspiracy theorist—especially the possibility that no matter how people vote, that Karl Rove's latest minions or Russians are prefiguring results. Yet in 2016, when almost everyone has been hacked, from the Pentagon to personal emails, and Volkswagen has preprogrammed emission systems to turn themselves off at smog tests, we can't pretend voting machines are magically immune.

Brakey—and a team including Silicon Valley coders and a retired National Security Agency analyst—discovered precincts near Milwaukee used cell-phone modems to send their results to county tabulators.

Why was the modem there? Because polls did not always have landline phones, officials said. The NSA analyst sent me links to commercial spyware used by police to intercept this data stream. Their point was Wisconsin's voting machines, like much of the nation, can easily be hacked. These vulnerabilities were identified more than a decade ago.

The Greens presented testimony from a half-dozen nationally known computer scientists saying these concerns were not a shrill conspiracy theory. Yet Wisconsin officials, echoing a stance taken in Pennsylvania—the third state where the Greens were told they would have to spend millions for a recount—ignored it. This wasn't just Republicans defending Trump. In Pennsylvania, Democrats oversee its elections. Helped by judges, they, too, shut the door on the Greens and blocked its recount. So more questions about the vote went unanswered. State and local officials thwarted inquires and evidence that could have assured the public.

The more I looked at various phases and features of the 2016 election, the more I saw a spectrum of antidemocratic features. That was also true at the process's start. It looked to me (and also to the *Des Moines Register* editorial page) like Sanders beat Clinton in Iowa's first-in-the-nation contest. I saw other tactics in Nevada, such as deciding where its caucuses were held and where they weren't, that made it easier for Clinton's supporters to participate. But beyond the anti-Sanders biases from top aides of DNC Chairwoman Debbie Wasserman Schultz, beyond scheduling televised candidate debates on weekends where audiences were smaller, and beyond shutting access to its national voter database as Sanders's grassroots donations soared, was the Democrats' antidemocratic super-delegate system.

These were 712 federal and state elected officials, party leaders, and lobbyists whose votes count toward the 2,384 needed for the presidential nomination. They preempt millions of citizens voting in caucuses and primaries. Most were with Clinton before Sanders entered the race and 570 stayed with her. Superdelegates are another example of a system filled with rules that privilege the few at the expense of many. This template keeps governing classes in place. But so, too, is who gets to vote, and whether those votes count.

What Democrats did to Sanders was nasty. But it pales next to what Republicans have done to Democrats and the vast majority of Americans. That is what was different about 2016 as well as every congressional and state election cycle since President Obama's election in 2008. It is what sets this decade apart, as a party representing a minority has seized power and steadily imposed a regime of oligarchy, plutocracy, and theocracy on its fellow citizens. It is one thing when Democrats run presidential nomination contests like private clubs with varying membership rules. But it is another when Republican strategists plot to win dozens of state legislatures and House seats, and then sabotage their critic's ability to compete in elections. The country is clearly living with the results of a subverted democracy.

Politics has always had hardball tactics, but as this introduction is being written in late 2017, Trump's national approval ratings were 35 percent. "Every party, gender, education, age, and racial group disapproves except Republicans," an August 23 Quinnipiac University poll reported. A week later, a poll by pro-Republican Fox News said 56 percent of voters "say Trump [is] tearing the country apart."[3]

Think about it, how can 2016's presidential election come down to less than eighty thousand votes in Wisconsin, Pennsylvania, and Michigan, yet two-thirds of the US House seats in those states—and even more seats in their legislatures—end up as red super-majorities? All things are not being equal. This same pattern is also found, with slight variations, in Florida, Georgia, North Carolina, Ohio, Virginia— all states where, if demographics were destiny, the political complexion should be purple turning blue or blue.

What's different now is the mechanisms of the Republican's advantage can be quantified. But you have to look carefully. Beyond all of 2016's headline-grabbing features—Trump's ugliness, Clinton's foibles, Sanders's populism, Russian meddling—what unfolded was the Democrats did not know what they were up against. They did not appreciate how rigged the process was—structurally stacked against them. Republicans had built in a starting-line lead of ten points or more. This isn't in every race. But it is enough of the ones that determine statewide rule in otherwise purple states and determines control of Congress. It also is seen in anti-voting laws and barriers in the presidential swing states.

There is no such thing as 50-percent-plus-one in high-stakes elections. To win in November, the party representing a majority of citizens needs very big margins that cannot be whittled away—as they will be whittled away. There is a wide and deeper dynamic operating here. But to see its entirety, we have to parse the details that comprise the voting process.

When I was drawn into the vortex of America's dysfunctional 2016 election via recounts, I did not think I'd emerge with an updated catalog of how the voting process preempts the citizenry and betrays democracy. It's so easy to be diverted into parallel concerns. That's especially true of the hope-deflating swamp of voting machine hacking, which, if it were widespread, renders all other efforts to improve the process futile. There are other big issues in the voting sphere, such as ex-felon disenfranchisement. That is why Florida is politically red, not blue. Florida's lifetime voting ban for its 1.6 million residents with a felony record, most nonviolent drug offenses, is a Jim Crow–era holdover.

Nonetheless, I keep coming back to a big picture where Democrats, progressives, and independents do not understand the fundamentals they are up against. In far too many states, Republicans have restructured the voting process in antidemocratic ways. The stakes are bigger for the country than the fate of which party or factions win and lose. The GOP has undermined the process that is the basis for representative government. Unless stakeholders, meaning citizens who put democracy before party, work to restore the voting process, the legitimacy of its outcomes will remain dubious and our political system will unravel.

This book is divided into four sections. It starts with the Democrats' nominating contests. The goal is not to rehash the Sanders-Clinton split within the party in 2016 and since. What Democratic national and state leadership threw at Sanders is a useful way to start looking at a landscape where insiders game the rules of voting. But even as these features undermine the Democrats' moral authority as the party that defends voting rights, their flaws are of a different and lesser caliber than the Republicans' attacks on voting in America.

The second section focuses on Republican efforts to disenfranchise opponents and preempt representative government. This section, the book's core, shows readers a range of strategies with their impact. As the nation looks ahead to elections in 2018 and 2020, what's new now is that the most pernicious tactics can be quantified. It's no longer a guessing game about which anti-voter laws and rules are the most harmful to citizens and voting.

The third section continues with the recount, where both major parties frustrated efforts to verify the vote count, and where the prospect of hacking was raised, insufficiently answered, and dismissed. (By mid-summer 2017 hacking resurfaced, although it appeared the Russian interventions were more impactful with hurting Democrats on social media than with the voting machinery.) The book concludes with an afterword focusing on 2017 and the Trump administration, where a rogues' gallery of Republicans have resurfaced in powerful posts and are poised to recycle their anti-voter playbook.

There is a way forward for Americans who seek a government that represents the nation's multiracial, multi-class, increasingly diverse citizenry. It starts with seeing what has happened to voting, how the process has been hijacked to subvert democracy, and acting to surmount it. Come take a look.

SECTION I
THE DEMOCRATS

1

BERNIE SANDERS

BERNIE SANDERS HAS ALWAYS BEEN A very able, savvy, and visceral politician. When I briefly had a front-row seat to Sanders, as press secretary on the campaign that first elected him to the House of Representatives in 1990, he was championing many of the same stances that resonated with millions in 2016. By the time he launched his presidential campaign in mid-2015, he was more of a political pro than anything I'd seen in Vermont decades before.

But neither Bernie nor his earliest supporters—practitioners of a "now I'm inside, now I'm outside" Democratic Party—nor his legions of youthful volunteers quite knew what they were getting into. They were taking on the Democratic Party's national establishment, state party leaders, a rickety election system, stone-faced administrators, political rituals manned by bungling locals, and, of course, the Clintons, now in their fourth presidential campaign. Bernie had never run for anything outside of Vermont. He had not faced real competition or dirty electioneering tactics in years. Nor had he interacted with the party insiders and others running caucuses and primaries, nor the vagaries of voting rules and administration.

Top campaign officials I spoke to in spring 2017 agreed that Bernie didn't know what he was getting into. But they said the Democratic Party didn't see him coming either, and as an institution it didn't respect the man, what he stood for, or his strengths as a candidate. The party's establishment had lost touch with its energized grassroots and younger base, which propelled a candidate who came out of nowhere to win 45 percent of the elected delegates to the Democratic National Convention.[4] But it was not the party's blindness, nor its insider-favoring rules alone that prevented Sanders from breaking through. There also were party traditions whose intent wasn't nefarious, but whose effects were antidemocratic.

Starting in 2015, Bernie had spoken at events set up by Progressive Democrats of America and others. Growing crowds clung to his words and embraced a refreshing and more blunt champion than Hillary Clinton. Bernie had a message that people wanted to hear and one he wanted to spread. Iowa's Caucuses, 2016's first testing ground, were in a state that was not that different from Vermont. It was mostly rural, white, and had progressive streaks.

But just because you want to run as a Democrat for president doesn't make it happen. You have to get on the ballot. The Democratic National Committee (DNC) didn't know what to make of his decision to seek their nomination. They knew of his old speeches condemning them and the GOP in one fell swoop. They also knew he had been a reliable Democratic vote for twenty-five years in the House and then the Senate. Mostly, they didn't take him seriously, just as they misread the loose energy on the land that is a feature of presidential elections. These are people who ditch their day jobs, throw caution to the wind, and join a political road show they deeply believe would change the nation and world.

Long after the party realized that Bernie was in it to win, and not just to hound members about their progressive populist past, I asked Debra Kozikowski, the Massachusetts Party vice-chair and a grass-roots activist for three decades, what had her peers been thinking? They backed putting Bernie on the ballot after he promised he would publicly support the 2016 nominee, she said. Their thinking was a calculated afterthought. They knew Bernie would bring along voters not drawn to Hillary. They thought he would boost her by a few points in key states. They never thought he would run neck and neck with the anointed nominee.

The first sign that Bernie was a very serious contender came in late 2015 when campaign finance reports were filed. Bernie was hardly the first progressive to reject donations from corporate PACs (political action committees) or newer deeper-pocket front groups, Super PACs. In 1992, ex-California Gov. Jerry Brown was mocked for announcing his 1-800 number for donations, but it worked. In 2016, Bernie used the Internet to raise nearly a quarter-billion dollars in funds averaging $27 per donation.[5] As late 2015's fund-raising reports were filed, the Clintons, and party insiders with signed photos of the Clintons on their desks, faced an intra-party split that was only deepening. The pro-Clinton party establishment would have to turn to hard(er) ball tactics to impede his candidacy.

The tension broke into public view in bizarre but telling ways. It's an example of barriers facing progressives, who wonder why there aren't more candidates like them in the party. The answer is because national leaders and pro-establishment liberals don't want them and haven't for years. This is the Clinton side of the party. These more traditional Democrats can be found in northeastern Virginia, New Jersey, Massachusetts, and even in California. By mid-fall 2015, the disputes between Bernie's surging grassroots campaign and Clinton allies inside the DNC began to break into the open.

The first frays were inside ball, but they revealed the DNC was privately operating as a subsidiary of the Clinton campaign (even if publicly posing as a neutral referee). In mid-October, Wikileaks—we now know, assisted by Russian intelligence agency hackers—posted an April 2015 memo from Charlie Baker, Clinton campaign chief administrative officer, to the Clinton campaign chairman, John Podesta.[6] It outlined the televised debate schedule that her camp wanted—and got. They were to be minimal, held on weekends when audiences were smaller, and were announced without input from Sanders.

By mid-December, the disputes reached a new orbit. As part of his candidacy, Sanders agreed to use the DNC's national voter database. Both major parties have these, where, in addition to all the public information from state voter registration files (name, address, party, etc.), the campaigns add tidbits like whether a voter likes their candidate, what issues matter to them, whether they will volunteer, and more. That information comes from phone calls and by going door-to-door by campaign workers. Bernie kept his donor list separate from the DNC, but his campaign had been using the party's voter file as they built a national organization.

Besides mutual feelings of distrust, there were accusations that Clinton's staffers, and then Sanders's staffers, had been spying on each other's voter files. DNC Chairwoman Debbie Wasserman Schultz responded by shutting off the Sanders campaign's access to the database in mid-December, at a time when Sanders was raking in millions from small grassroots donations daily. Groups like MoveOn launched petitions. The Sanders campaign sued the DNC before cooler heads prevailed.[7] The episode, nonetheless, cemented its belief the party was all in for Hillary.

These brazen attempts to tip the scales were precursors to what unfolded in the first electoral contests involving voters—the party caucuses and primary elections. Even more examples surfaced as the nominating season ended, when Wikileaks released stolen emails from top DNC staff with anti-Bernie plots, including possible lines of attack. Those came as Clinton loyalists fumed that Sanders was not conceding and had the audacity to keep campaigning through the convention. They forget that Clinton kept pushing similarly in 2008 to regain delegates she lost in Florida and Michigan after those states unilaterally moved up their primaries and were penalized by the DNC. Some of these behaviors and reactions were due to the emotional turmoil found on every presidential campaign. But there were other ways state parties and the DNC rigged their voting rules.

Sanders was more than aware of the DNC's biggest insider bias: its superdelegate system. This is where 713 of 2,383 national convention

voters—to nominate their 2016 presidential candidate—were prese-
lected Democratic elected officials, state party leaders, loyalists, and
lobbyists. Superdelegates only exist for one purpose: to take the nomination away from duly cast primary votes and caucuses. While party
brass said that has not happened, and in fact would never happen,
their existence is not merely an antidemocratic facet of its way of doing
business. Superdelegates undermine the Democrats' moral authority
to criticize the blatant and often racist efforts by the GOP to disenfranchise voters, especially nonwhites in blue epicenters.

Sanders downplayed the DNC's affirmative action for insiders,
believing these Democrats would back him if he won the popular vote
in the caucuses and primaries. But unlike Bill and Hillary Clinton, his
team had yet to compete in these contests, let alone master each state's
intricacies where party loyalists intentionally acted and deprived him
of victories. That inside edge surfaced in the very first contest, the Iowa
caucuses in late January.

2

WHO WON IOWA?

BERNIE HAD EVERY REASON TO BE upbeat about Iowa. He followed a trail blazed by George McGovern in 1972 and Jimmy Carter in 1976. After Democrats had a disastrous 1968 convention in Chicago, where Democratic Mayor Richard Daley ordered city police to crack down on anti-Vietnam War protesters, the DNC was forced to respond to entirely accurate accusations that their power brokers controlled the nomination process. They responded by moving Iowa's grassroots caucuses to its first-in-the-nation position.[8]

McGovern, a senator from nearby South Dakota, didn't win Iowa's 1972 caucuses, even though his antiwar platform eventually brought him the nomination. However, Carter, a relatively unknown governor from Georgia, started showing up in Iowa in 1974 and set the precedent followed by most candidates since. He went from town to town, stopping in diners, giving speeches before local civic clubs, recruiting volunteers, appearing on local media, and ignoring the national press, which dismissed anyone they disliked. Two years later, Carter was the nominee and then the next president. After he lost the 1980 election to Ronald Reagan, a DNC commission reinstated superdelegates to make sure an outsider like him was never nominated again.[9]

Bernie moved to northeastern Vermont four years before the Chicago debacle. Like other 1960s countercultural types, he was an urban intellectual refugee drawn to a state whose rural lifestyle was punctuated by short summers, long winters, mud seasons, hardscrabble farming, and voting for Republican presidents. He fell in with the proud but tolerant locals, a mix of personal libertarians, neighborly socialists, and antiestablishment types. His tell-it-like-it-is—but never lie—style worked. Old Vermonters touted their self-reliance, but they knew what life was like before Franklin Delano Roosevelt's New Deal brought electricity to their farms. The natives may not have liked Bernie's politics, but they knew where he stood. They respected his consistency and, over time, started voting for him.

Nearly a half century later when Bernie began campaigning in Iowa, he was more than at home. He even had an advantage that Clinton did not. He was new; a Socialist novelty who quickly showed he was a dogged campaigner and dead serious on issues. The last socialist candidate who ignited as big a grassroots movement was Eugene Debs, who had long inspired Sanders. Debs ran for president a century ago, including once from a jail cell, after Democratic president Woodrow Wilson had him arrested for demanding peace and social justice.[10]

Everything Sanders had going for him, from his moral compass to his passionate delivery to his long-distance runner stamina from an athletic youth, served him well. As the Iowa's caucuses approached, his campaign estimated that he had held more than a hundred rallies and town meetings and had spoken to seventy thousand people.[11] His staff was filled with supporters who would not be put off by participating in that wintery event, including young techies who devised apps to track voting.

What Bernie's campaign didn't have, notwithstanding the loyalty among Iowans that the Clintons had built up over the decades, was the support of the Iowa Democratic Party's top leaders. Nor did his burgeoning campaign have an understanding of how chaotic, opaque, and unaccountable the caucus process could be. Vermonters were familiar with their state's presidential caucuses and town meetings, where, after debate and huddling in the corners of libraries and gymnasiums, the winners and issues are openly decided. But that's not what unfolded in 2016's opening contest where the coverage and messaging would be critical.

What unfolded on caucus night was as predictable as it was offensive to participants and observers who expect our democracy to be fair, transparent, and accountable. As the results started pouring in, Sanders and Clinton were running neck and neck. Other Democrats, like Maryland's ex-Gov. Martin O'Malley, were behind. The Sanders team used its app to report local results to headquarters, while the caucus chairs were calling in or using a Microsoft app from the party. As results started adding up, so did complaints about the process.

"Too many questions have been raised," was how the editorial writers at Iowa's foremost newspaper, the *Des Moines Register*, put it days later. "Too many accounts have arisen of inconsistent counts, untrained and overwhelmed volunteers, confused voters, cramped precinct locations, a lack of voter registration forms and other problems. Too many of us, including members of the *Register* editorial board who were observing caucuses, saw opportunities for error amid Monday night's chaos."[12]

Let's pause there. Opportunities for error, coming after the DNC colluded with Clinton in the debates and tried to impede Sanders's fund-raising, begin to show how winning is not simply a matter of getting 50 percent plus one. To win in modern America, whether as a Democratic Party presidential contender in a state party caucus or in a general election against Republicans, requires specific margins, given the rules of the contest at hand.

The Iowa caucuses winner was not who won the popular vote, but who won the most delegates to the next stage in the process, its state party convention. As Jonathan Allen and Amie Parnes wrote in their book, *Shattered: Inside Hillary Clinton's Doomed Campaign*, Iowa's caucuses were "a math exercise that didn't necessarily require Clinton to win more total votes but to take a majority at the right set of caucus sites."[13]

Clinton's campaign knew this. They positioned themselves to quickly declare victory. At 2:30 AM on Tuesday, February 2, Iowa Democratic Party Chairwoman Andy McGuire announced that Clinton had won 699.57 "state delegate equivalents" to the next stage in the process, while Sanders had won 695.49 "state delegate equivalents." Only one precinct out of 1,682 across Iowa had not reported. That locale, Des Moines No. 42, where Sanders won, was presided by a voter who only agreed to do so after showing up late and was unaware he had to report the results that night. Five minutes after McGuire's announcement, Matt Paul, Clinton's Iowa director, issued a statement claiming victory and declaring nothing would change it. Her campaign staff was in full giant-killing mode.

"Hillary Clinton has won the Iowa caucus," Paul said. "After thorough reporting—and analysis—of results, there is no uncertainty and Secretary Clinton has clearly won the most national and state delegates. Statistically, there is no outstanding information that could change the results and no way that Senator Sanders can overcome Secretary Clinton's advantage."[14]

That no outstanding information claim was a lie and Iowa's politicos knew it. The headline of the *Register's* analysis was, "Iowa's Nightmare Revisited: Was Correct Winner Called?"[15] Four years earlier, Mitt Romney was named the GOP winner, but an audit of the counties showed Rick Santorum had more votes—along with finding that some precincts had not reported. However, unlike Iowa Republicans, McGuire and her party rejected an audit and refused to release the raw vote counts. The party wouldn't budge from its opaque delegate-allocation math. Clinton's victory would stand.

The *Register* editorialized but got nowhere. "Something smells in the Democratic Party," it wrote, fingering McGuire, who "dug in her heels." A two-tenths of 1 percent difference between candidates would "trigger automatic recounts in other states," it wrote, hoping a reasoned argument might have traction. "Her path forward is clear: Work with all the campaigns to audit results. Break silly party tradition and release the raw vote totals. Provide a list of each precinct coin flip [when candidates tied] and its outcome, as well as other information sought by the Register. Be transparent."[16]

By the time McGuire made her announcement, both Sanders and Clinton had left the state. Both were headed to New Hampshire for the nation's first primary, where voters cast ballots and every vote is counted equally. "I can tell you, I've won and I've lost there, and it's a lot better to win," Clinton said the next day. Sanders, in his post-2016 book, *Our Revolution*, didn't say anything about Iowa's antidemocratic tally or its flawed caucus process.

"Most of the media correctly perceived the night as a victory for us," he wrote. "From the first day of the campaign, we knew that we would have to do well in the early states to establish credibility and let the world know that we were in this for the long haul."[17]

Bernie's retelling took the high road. His campaign manager, Jeff Weaver, started to say that he was "the most electable Democrat," a line he would repeat throughout the spring. Weaver may have been right. But Iowa's caucus was not an election, per se. It was a high-stakes process where those at the helm in precincts—doing it the way it has always been done—were more likely to be incompetent than corrupt.

At the state party level, there was a different intransigence: a system of counting that is not the equivalent of one person, one vote. Should anyone have been surprised that Iowa's party hid behind math to help Clinton, not someone who had not been a Democrat until running for president?

This is hardball, not the fair, rational process the *Register's* editorial page sought. Anyone doing homework should have seen this coming. In 2008, Clinton's campaign made a similar move when it stretched the truth to say it had won Texas—which national media reported—even though Obama later emerged as the victor. Democrats in Texas cast ballots in a two-step process: a primary during the day and caucus at night. Clinton won the primary. But Obama won the caucuses. As reporters waited for her speech in Columbus, Ohio—also holding its primary that day—her campaign ludicrously said tens of thousands of Texans may have illegally caucused for Obama. That baseless accusation finessed her victory declaration in two states that night, which she needed to try to blunt Obama.[18]

After Iowa's caucuses, Clinton's campaign panicked. With the help of allies in the DNC, they added an unscheduled televised debate before New Hampshire's primary. That broke the schedule they helped write and refused to budge on a few months before. But the extra debate didn't help Clinton and probably further legitimized Sanders's stature. He won New Hampshire, Vermont's eastern neighbor. Weaver kept saying that Sanders was the most electable Democrat. But what Sanders's campaign would soon find out in the next state they needed to win was there were other fine-print rules and barriers to a fair contest.

3

LAS VEGAS RULES

SANDERS HAD ONE BIG CHANCE TO upset the Clinton campaign before the race headed to South Carolina and then to early March's Super Tuesday, where eleven mostly southern and central states were expected to deliver for Clinton. That was Nevada, a western state with a racially diverse population centered in Las Vegas to the south and Reno to the north. Nevada is not a wealthy state. But it is nothing like Iowa and New Hampshire. It is more like California, a mix of rustic downtowns and sprawling suburbs and residential neighborhoods. Las Vegas was home to a very powerful union, the Culinary Workers local, whose fifty-eight thousand members, mostly Latino and black, work in the corporate-run hotel, casino, and hospitality industry.

Bernie hadn't spent as much time in Nevada as he had Iowa and New Hampshire. In *Our Revolution*, he said that was the right choice because he had to make a strong start to be taken seriously as a candidate. By the time Nevada's mid-February caucuses came, he'd held seventeen events in the state, including a large outdoor rally at the University of Nevada in Reno. On Election Day, he stopped by Culinary Workers picket lines in Las Vegas and visited hotels and casinos along the strip, including some where the Nevada Democratic Party had set up caucus sites in rooms normally used for conventions. Bill and Hillary Clinton also made the rounds, visiting employee lounges and urging workers to vote.

Like Iowa, Nevada's Democratic Party ran the caucuses according to their rules. It had an obscure delegate allocation formula and
multistep nominating process that began at local precincts, moved to
county, and then to state conventions. Sanders ran into obstacles not
seen in Iowa and New Hampshire. These were institutional decisions
that affected who would likely participate and how easy that would—
or not—affect voter turnout. It well may have been that despite growing momentum, he was not going to beat Clinton as he had run out of
time to have become known in the state where no candidate goes town
to town, or holds forth in diners and civic clubs. But his chances would
have been better if the Nevada Party—and its true leader, Senator
Harry Reid—had played fairer and squarer.

Jon Ralston, the Nevada press corps dean, recounted in a *USA
Today* commentary how the party rescued Clinton.[19] Ralston said Reid,
the retiring Senate Minority Leader, claimed he was neutral but was
working for a nervous Clinton camp. First, Reid told the Las Vegas
Culinary Workers Union president not to endorse a candidate. He
agreed and predicted his members would skip the vote. Then, Reid lob-
bied casinos to let the workers get time off to caucus. He then pushed
the union to deploy "swarms of organizers to turn out mostly Latino
workers, who would likely vote for Clinton." I was at one of the casino
sites and saw waves of employees arrive just before the cut-off time to
participate. Most, especially women, said they were for Clinton. When
asked why, several replied that if she were in trouble, Hillary's husband
would tell her what to do.

Ralston said the credibility of "Prince Harry" was on the line and
he delivered a result "that could indeed prove to be a contest that saved
Clinton's campaign." The rescue was a good story and surely contained
elements of the truth. But it doesn't note what else happened that
added to Clinton's victory on February 20. Out of the eighty thousand
or so participants statewide, the party said Clinton had won 52.64 percent of the delegates to the county forums while Sanders won 47.29
percent. One vote doesn't equal one delegate equivalent in the party's

math, but there were not more than twenty-five hundred participants at the six Las Vegas casino precincts. What Ralston didn't say, but what was in Reno newspapers, was a laundry list of factors that could tilt close elections.

Nevada Party leaders know that whoever won Las Vegas would win the state. So what did they do for which Sanders had no recourse and was beyond Reid's efforts? First, the party's caucuses are closed to voters who are not registered as Democrats. Closed primaries are not unique to Nevada, but they prevent last-minute enthusiasts or independents from participating if they didn't register as Democrats. The party also had no caucus sites at Las Vegas universities, a setting where Sanders was likely to draw supporters. In Reno, there were caucus sites on campuses, which contributed to Sanders winning northern Nevada despite other snafus.[20]

The *Reno Gazette Journal*'s coverage two days later categorized the problems they has witnessed.[21] These included: "strange delegate math," "long check-in process," "wrong location," "people who left were improperly counted," "people with disabilities not allowed to exercise rights," "disorganized and unprofessional," "Clinton voters allowed to break rules," "Wi-Fi overload," "text check-in not working," "cards not counted," "voters turned away." These complications, which are not unique to Nevada's caucuses, refer to various steps in the process. This list deserves closer scrutiny.

These factors, some due to incompetence and others due to institutional decisions, make participating easier or harder. Some help or hurt specific constituents, such as location. Then there are other ways of deterring voters and eroding turnout, from poor planning that leads to long check-in lines at precincts to overcrowding and inexperienced staffing. Those are all details the state party should anticipate and address. Not doing so in Nevada in 2016, a year where one-third fewer Democrats caucused compared to the 2008 Clinton-Obama race, suggests the party either intended Reno's voting to be messy or it should not be running caucuses. Many academics drew the latter conclusion.

The problem with barriers to participation is they stay below the radar until it's too late. Come Election Day, especially in close races, complaining goes nowhere. After Iowa's and Nevada's opening caucuses, Sanders's campaign wised up. They knew the voting and count weren't straightforward or precise. On April 2, when the party's county conventions were held, only two-thirds of the delegates elected in February showed up: 2,964 for Sanders, and 2,386 for Clinton. Sanders ended that day by sending 1,613 delegates to the state convention, while Clinton sent 1,298.[22]

That turnaround prompted Sanders's campaign to tweet that they had staged a comeback. But they hadn't. By that time, the campaign press wasn't following steps between the first caucuses and national party convention, except for pages dedicated to delegate counts. Sanders's surge didn't make much news. Moreover, his win was among the elected delegates, not the DNC's superdelegates. His Nevada campaign won a key battle but lost the war.

I briefly ran into Weaver the night before opening caucuses. The campaign held a rally at an amphitheater in Henderson, east of Las Vegas. I had not seen him in decades. We agreed no one who knew Bernie back then could have imagined that he would be running for president and become a real contender. Weaver hoped the campaign would squeak out a Nevada win and confided that the next stretch of states—South Carolina and southern states on Super Tuesday—would go for Clinton. But after that, he said there would be a month or more where everything should line up behind Bernie.

That's what happened. But in key states where primary elections ensued, their campaign ran into other antidemocratic hurdles. Some came from state party policies. Some came from administrative blunders and stonewalling by local election officials. Some were by media coverage and discouraged turnout. All of these hurdles underscore that nobody, especially outsiders like Bernie, can win unless they generate turnout that becomes a wave big enough to breach the barriers. The contest's next phase illustrated this point again and again.

4

NEW QUESTIONS,
NEW BARRIERS

FROM SUPER TUESDAY IN EARLY MARCH until late April's primary in New York, the pendulum swung from Clinton's recovery in the South to a Sanders surge in the Midwest and West, where he won seven primaries and caucuses in a row. Clinton's streak, the first part of that progression, was unsurprising. But her pattern of repeatedly outperforming Election Day media exit polls did not sit well with election integrity activists who saw foul play in the discrepancies between the exit polls and official results.

Their suspicions kept rising after exit polls forecasting Clinton's victory were off by more than ten points in South Carolina, Alabama, and Georgia; and by slightly less in Tennessee, and in Democratic strongholds in Missouri, Illinois, and Ohio. (When the nominating season ended, these data-crunching activists found other odd patterns, such as Sanders winning in smaller precincts where ballots were counted by hand but losing in larger ones where votes were tallied electronically.) To them, this points to hacking or altering counts by tampering with voting machine software.[23] Party leaders and election officials routinely ignore these discrepancies and complaints, and officials never let anyone examine their voting systems. Candidates also stay away. Sanders avoided this issue entirely in his campaign book.

I'm averse for other reasons. I know hacking is possible, respect academics who have shown how it can be done, and suspect it has happened in races where fewer people are watching, such as in local noncandidate bond issues. But I have not seen sufficient proof in my years of covering federal elections. That doesn't mean it's not out there somewhere. But all we see are patterns that raise questions that are never sufficiently answered. After a point, I return to more tangible and traceable factors that shape elections and voting. Sanders kept facing these more concrete partisan barriers and administrative oopsies that consistently favored Clinton as the race unfolded.

His book mentions how mistakes by county election officials— beyond antidemocratic state party rules—also affected thousands of voters. These are in a different class than bungling precinct captains, incompetent state party chairs, and antidemocratic party rules. These are less excusable because these are coming from government officials on public payrolls.

One of the foremost examples was in Arizona's largest county, Maricopa, where Phoenix is located. Its top election official, Helen Purcell, who had held that post for years, made a bad judgment call when she closed 140 out of 200 voting centers for the primary. It is likely she never would have been allowed to do this had the enforcement trigger in the 1965 Voting Rights Act had not been declared unconstitutional by the Supreme Court in 2013.[24] The Justice Department had previously questioned having one poll for every 21,000 voters, compared to an average of 2,500 for the rest of the state. What could go wrong?

Purcell, like many administrators, sought to make voting more efficient. Her mistake was implementing this in a presidential primary and not a lower-turnout race. To say that voters were caught off-guard is an understatement. People didn't know where to vote. Some stood in line for five-plus hours to get into the voting centers. Local activists, national civil rights law groups, Sanders, Clinton, and the DNC all filed lawsuits. One suit sought to throw out the primary results.

Another challenged Purcell's rationale but also took aim at other anti-voter tactics, such as a 2016 state law making it a felony to collect another person's ballot and bring it to a poll (making it harder for Native Americans and seniors). Another wanted the county's elections under court supervision. Nothing changed the results in the jurisdiction where 70 percent of Arizona's Latinos live.[25]

Sanders mentioned this morass in his book, saying he was stunned by how an administrative decision undermined the finish line of a hard-fought campaign. "I thought we had a good shot to win there. We didn't and I still don't know why. One thing I do know was that the voting process in Arizona was an absolute disaster and an embarrassment to American democracy," he wrote. "Nobody can ever really know which candidate was hurt more by this travesty, but I don't think it helped us. Many of Clinton's supporters were older and voted by mail. Most of our supporters came out on Election Day with the obvious expectation that they would be allowed to vote in a reasonable period of time."[26]

The Sanders campaign would soon discover that sloppy election administration could be as damaging to his efforts as antidemocratic state party rules. As his April momentum grew, the media's eyes turned to New York and the Big Apple where many news outlets are based. Its April 19 primary had every angle for maximum drama. A Brooklyn-born socialist returned home to face the state's former two-term US senator, who also was the former secretary of state and First Lady. Hovering below this hype was a big blue state's notoriously stubborn Democratic Party and intransigent election officials.

The primary run by the New York State Democratic Committee is one of two dozen in the United States that are closed, meaning only registered Democrats can participate.[27] Like Nevada, independents or voters who joined another party cannot make a last-minute decision to cast a vote for a Democrat that will count. They might show up and insist on voting, but they will get a provisional ballot after not being listed as a Democrat. Their ballot will not count when counties finalize their tallies. New York's closed primaries meant three million Independents could not cast a vote for Sanders, even though he was elected as one to Congress for more than a quarter century.

That wasn't the worst of it. New York has the nation's longest party registration deadlines.[28] It's been this way for decades and nobody in power is inclined to change it. To vote in the Democrats' April 2016 primary, you would have had to register as a party member by October 2015. So even as Bernie held rallies before tens of thousands across New York City, many people who heard and liked him could not vote for him.[29] If that wasn't frustrating enough, another barrier emerged in a key borough targeted by his campaign. As April began, news broke that the Board of Elections (BOE) in Kings County, better known as Brooklyn, had purged—or removed—122,000 voters from the official rolls, and had not told those people they could not vote in the primary.[30]

The rough outline of what happened merits explaining. These nuts and bolts are some of what Republicans seize and distort when they make claims about voter fraud, their made-up menace and excuse for passing anti-voter laws in red states. Basically, Brooklyn's election office failed to keep their voter rolls current, and was slammed in public reports for things that sounded worse than they were—but it still kept messy bookkeeping. Then the county's Board of Elections (BOE) made matters worse by locally purging voters but not telling the state's election agency—whose online records said those people could vote in 2016's primary.

The problem that kept Brooklyn's voter rolls from being accurate is one faced by every county in America. After registered voters move, marry and change their names, or die, almost nobody notifies local election offices. Thus, voter rolls, which are not magically updated, are in a state of flux because a county's demographics are constantly changing. Some states have reliable data systems that track and update these changes, but not New York State and not Brooklyn. Dead people can remain listed, as well as people who move and register elsewhere.

The dead don't vote. Neither do most people who move, although there's always a handful—usually in single digits—who think they can vote in more than one state. Voter roll errors are an easy target for sensation-seeking media that don't think through what they are writing. The GOP also targets outdated lists as it looks to overly police the process, usually by creating impediments to blue voting blocs.

Before the 2016 primary, a New York City government audit report hit Brooklyn hard for its sloppiness in voter-list maintenance. Then Kings County didn't follow the steps of a 1993 law (the National Voter Registration Act) that laid out how voter purges are to be done.[31] That law said that nobody who is a registered voter can be purged unless they have not voted in two federal cycles—four years—and not until after county offices try to contact them about losing their voting rights. That was where the BOE began to screw up, because they found 122,000 people who had not voted since 2008, purged them from rolls starting in 2015, but did not tell the state's election agency. When New Yorkers went to the state's website, they saw that they could vote. However, they couldn't. All this surfaced on April Fools' Day.

The result on April 19 was confusion, frustration, and anger as large numbers of people showed up and found they were not listed as voters, or their party affiliation was incorrect—another bureaucratic snafu—and they couldn't vote in the primary they wanted. As is typical in New York, local officials barely budged. A handful of voters went to court, and, helped by election protection attorneys, won the right to cast a regular ballot. Most did not. New York State's Attorney General Eric Schneiderman said his office received over a thousand complaints.[32] The county BOE director, Michael Ryan, declared that, "no one was disenfranchised." That's absurd, not after 120,000 Brooklyn voters cast provisional ballots, of which only 31,000 ended up being counted. The rest were deemed ineligible.

New York was the latest big race that Sanders needed to win to blunt Clinton's lead. His campaign threw everything they had at it, including most of their media budget. He also flew to the Vatican to see the pope days before the primary. But it did not happen. Even if all of those voided Brooklyn votes had gone for Sanders, he would have fallen short by more than 100,000 votes statewide. Berniecrats correctly pointed out partisan barriers (closed primaries, registration deadline) and administrative snafus (voter roll purges and other errors) were not confined to Kings County. New York being New York, finger pointing ensued. Brooklyn officials were disciplined. Lawsuits ensued—including the Department of Justice intervening in early 2017. But the primary results remained.

Months later, Sanders wrote, "We worked very hard there and ran an excellent campaign, but there were just too many obstacles in our way." He forged on and looked to the last big blue state, California, to try to make a case to the DNC superdelegates that he was more electable than Clinton.[33] Like every key state before it, California presented yet more obstacles that he didn't anticipate.

5

THE NOT-SO-GOLDEN STATE

AFTER LOSING NEW YORK, DELAWARE, PENNSYLVANIA, Maryland, and Connecticut—but winning in Rhode Island, Indiana, West Virginia, and Oregon—Sanders's campaign made a strategic decision. They would shut operations in other states and tell their best organizers to go to California. Its June 7 primary fell on the last day of all state nominating contests. By then, Sanders had won 45 percent of the pledged delegates. He felt that if they won the biggest state, they might sway the superdelegates. National and state polls kept reporting he was doing better than Clinton in theoretical matchups with Trump.

Sanders then did what no presidential candidate has done in decades. He spent a month in California, holding forty rallies that brought out nearly a quarter-million people.[34] Like New York, California had different quirky procedures and party rules regarding who could and could not vote in their primary. California's confusion began when voters were asked if they wanted to join a party on the state registration form. There are a series of boxes to check. The first was "American Independent Party," a right-wing party, which is not an independent. Tens of thousands of Californians inadvertently joined the AIP.

They should have checked the "No Party Preference" (NPP) box.

But that wasn't clear. The *Los Angeles Times* estimated three-quarters of AIP's members had zero intention of joining it—half a million people.[35] That error set in motion a series of dominoes that fell as voting began, first by mail-in ballots and then at precincts. The California Democratic Party allows NPP voters, genuine independents, to vote in its primary, unlike New York.[36] But people who thought they were independents and wanted to vote by mail received the AIP primary ballot. A similar situation unfolded at the polls.[37] California's Democratic Party, led by Gov. Jerry Brown who backed Clinton, did not say anything to clear up this confusion.

Still, Sanders was upbeat. The crowds at his rallies were big and enthusiastic, and ignored East Coast media calls for him to drop out. He had run out of money for statewide advertising—which costs millions per week in California. Nonetheless, Clinton took him seriously and returned for a final series of rallies and fund-raisers.

Then one of 2016's most inglorious moments of media bias struck. One day before the primary, the Associated Press published an article saying its team had reached all of the undeclared superdelegates and found Clinton had secured the nomination.[38] To declare the race over less than twenty-four hours before millions of Californians were to vote in the first primary that mattered in their state in decades was the height of arrogance. The AP is not any wire service. It's a national co-op whose reports become the basis for local TV and radio news, and whose articles fill the pages of regional and local newspapers.

There is no way to quantify the impact of the AP's ambush of 2016's final primaries. It was an unforeseen antidemocratic deed in a season marred by them. Sanders wrote in his book, "I strongly believe that their action had a negative impact on voter turnout and hurt us. Why vote if the election was over? Our younger voters were more likely to cast their votes on Election Day rather than voting earlier by absentee ballot, as many Clinton voters did."[39]

On Primary Day, California also experienced its share of administrative snafus that never seem to disappear in American elections. Poll workers gave out provisional ballots instead of regular ones. Some polls had incomplete voter rolls. Some ran out of paper ballots. That night, the media announced that Clinton had won by fourteen points, more than exit polls had forecast. She also won in New Jersey, New Mexico, and South Dakota, while Sanders won Montana and North Dakota.

The last primaries ended Sanders's presidential hopes. Had he won a majority of elected delegates, he planned to file a series of motions as the Democratic National Convention's opening gavel fell to disqualify superdelegates, and then quickly move to a vote based on pledged delegates. At that point, Sanders would have either won the nomination or walked out, a senior campaign aide told me in spring 2017. This strategy was not reported at the time.

Within a week of the last primaries, however, Sanders and his senior staff began meeting with Clinton to negotiate what the party would do to honor his issues; in the platform, party rules (reforming the superdelegate system) and with campaigning that fall. Those meetings began before California finished its official vote count. That took time because California uses paper ballots counted by scanners, and millions of mailed-in ballots. Once the count was done, he had 46 percent, cutting her supposed primary night lead in half.[40]

Bernie's month of campaigning in California and the state's party's rules of letting independents vote in its primary made a difference, though not enough for him to win. That is a much-overlooked capstone to his performance in California. Think about it: starting with Iowa's caucuses, Sanders encountered a series of state party rules and other decisions that favored his opponent and did little to embrace the millions of voters who were drawn to him. The voters who sent 45 percent of elected delegates to Philadelphia's convention were underestimated, underrepresented, and marginalized by their party's leaders.

On top of that, Sanders faced the institutional clumsiness of the voting process. In caucus states, inept precinct captains and states' chairs were not up to the task of running contests with presidential nominations at stake. In primary states, many key elements overseen by county government officials—registration deadlines, voter list maintenance and purges, precinct locations, voter lists—complicated rather than clarified voting, especially for first-time voters and independents. Together, what Sanders and his base experienced was that winning takes much more than embracing a candidate you believe in.

6

THE DEMOCRATIC NATIONAL COMMITTEE

But the biggest barrier to Sanders breaking through was the party culture and its leaders. These are political pros that know better, know what nefarious behavior is and isn't, and whose biases blinded them to not just Sanders but to the party's antidemocratic rules.

When DNC Chairwoman Debbie Wasserman Schultz was interviewed in February 2016 by CNN after Iowa and New Hampshire, she fiercely defended the superdelegate system.[41] They "exist really to make sure that party leaders and elected officials don't have to be in a position where they are running against grassroots activists," she said. Wasserman Schultz did not see superdelegates as affirmative action for insiders, but said they were to ensure that diverse constituencies have a say in the party. Superdelegates have never departed from primary and caucus results, she said, and chosen a different nominee. This breezy explanation ducked the bigger issues at play, including her loyalty to Clinton.

In politics, real motives are usually not what is said in public. On the weekend before the Democratic National Convention opened in Philadelphia, Wasserman Schultz was forced to resign after WikiLeaks released emails from her top staff showing plots to attack Sanders—such as questioning his religious beliefs.[42] This was the last straw, because, even if Hillary loyalists smoldered that Sanders had refused to warmly endorse her after California, it told Sanders's supporters, nearly half the party, that they were to be stepped on and sidelined.[43]

Of course, the DNC's bias was evident before the first votes were cast. Beyond its superdelegates, most of whom were Clinton supporters before Iowa and stayed that way, were other candidate-centered aggressions and antidemocratic slights. The DNC cut off Sanders's access to its national voter database as his fundraising peaked in late 2015. It scheduled debates on weekends, when fewer people would become familiar with him as a candidate and his policies, as well as his critiques of Clinton. The DNC created a joint fund-raising effort with the Clinton campaign before the 2016 nominee was known. WikiLeaks showed that Donna Brazile, the ex-DNC chair who was then a CNN analyst, shared debate questions with the Clinton campaign before its primary debate.[44] Incredibly, Brazile took the DNC helm after Wasserman Schultz resigned in disgrace.

Another open admission came in February 2017 when the soon-to-be elected DNC chairman, Obama's former labor secretary Tom Perez, told Kansas lawmakers that 2016 was rigged from the inside. "We heard loudly and clearly yesterday from Bernie supporters that the process was rigged, and it was," Perez said. "You've got to be honest about it. That's why we need a chair who is transparent." Needless to say, Perez immediately got flack for that honesty and later tweeted that he "misspoke."[45]

The notion that political ends justify the means, and doing whatever it takes is loyal and patriotic, is as old as politics itself. But the modern Democratic Party is supposed to be the party fighting voter suppression, not deploying it. It is the party that keeps going into court to defend voting rights from Republican attacks. To run its presidential nominating contest as inside ball violates what the party says it stands for. Take Wasserman Schultz's defense of superdelegates to ensure minority representation. That definition excluded the grassroots, which, as it turned out, were up for grabs in 2016 and which Trump deftly exploited.

Sanders chose his words carefully when he discussed voter suppression in his post-2016 book. As you would expect, he first noted how Supreme Court campaign finance rulings have empowered billionaires to single-handedly finance candidates. But Sanders then turned to the Court's 2013 gutting of the Voting Rights Act. That 1965 law was passed after many states, mostly in the South, adopted rules to keep blacks from voting. However, the Supreme Court's Republican-appointed majority, led by Chief Justice John Roberts, said voter suppression was no longer a problem that required the federal government to sign off on any new election law or procedure in covered states. In response, GOP-run states moved very quickly to pass a series of laws making it harder for Democrats to vote.

Sanders is unsparing in his criticism of those who would rig the rules rather than win by the power of their ideas. "Political cowards are doing everything they can to keep people from voting," he wrote. "They are making it harder for people to register and to participate in the political process."[46]

Many of the things that Sanders correctly criticizes the GOP for—creating voting barriers, hiding behind opaque rules and procedures, failing to ensure election administration is fully modernized and professional, and ensuring accurate and verifiable counts—have analogues in the Democrats' nominating process. While the Republicans are far more accomplished in the dark arts of undermining voting and elections, one has to wonder if voters experiencing a more open Democratic contest would bring about fairer and more accountable elections.

"Democracy should be easy," Sanders wrote. "All adults must have the right to vote. We can and should spend the money necessary to defend democracy by making sure polling places are adequately staffed, that voting machines function well, and that however voting is tabulated, there are paper ballots that can be counted and audited in cases where the voting is close or contested."[47]

That sounds simple, but it isn't simple in a nation where our constitutional system has its roots and retains key characteristics of the late 1700s, when slavery, racism, classism, sexism, and other hard lines enshrined economic elites, while excluding those who challenge that order.

Today, there is a party that believes the country does not benefit when every eligible adult votes and unapologetically keeps passing laws and adopting rules in that antidemocratic spirit. That is the Republicans. Its path to power starts with creating red-state monopolies and extends to dominating the US House and presidential swing states. Until their game plan and tactics are understood, unmasked, and bested, a minority party that consistently elicits fewer popular votes nationally, will not be relegated to history.

SECTION II
THE REPUBLICANS

7

GAMING THE RULES
OF POLITICS

IT'S TIME TO SET ASIDE THE notion that American democracy is based
on free and fair elections, epitomized by one-person–one-vote. Instead,
we need to recognize the frame that the nation's founders created: a
system that elevates elites and manipulates the rules of voting to shape
outcomes.[48] This legacy endures today, despite twentieth-century US
Supreme Court decisions affirming the ideal of one person, one vote.

Perhaps the best-known example of this enduring legacy is the
Senate. Wyoming, with less than six hundred thousand residents, has
the same representation as California with 37 million residents. Another
is the Constitution's Three-Fifths Clause in Article 1, which allocated
House seats based on a state's population and counted slaves as three-
fifths of a person. Historians have noted that ugly formula gave more
clout to slave states via overrepresentation.[49] But its shadow continues
today in the Electoral College, where each state's president-selecting
vote is based on its congressional delegation's size. Tinkering with
underlying rules for elections by insiders acting on "superior knowl-
edge" and "sufficient virtue" is as old as America. It just takes new
forms: some more obvious and some more odious.

In American politics, there have always been factions who argue

that allowing free and fair elections invites mob rule.[50] That's why
the state legislatures appointed the US Senate (almost uniformly
wealthy white men) until the Seventeenth Amendment was enacted
in 1913. There are right-wingers today that want to go back to that
way of selecting US senators,[51] just as House members like Florida
Republican Ted Yolo believe that only property owners should vote.
Pundits and scholars say politics has always been this way: whoever
holds power will publicly offer high-minded words about democratic
principles, but behind closed doors use every available advantage to
game the system's operating rules. To expect anything else is naive.

Most political reporting looks at the results in elections, not the
underlying "porous and partisan" structures, rules, and administration that feed into the outcomes, as voting rights attorney Michael
Waldman described it in his 2016 book, *The Fight to Vote*.[52] Yet, in
order to understand why the nation has had the Republican-majority
House and red supermajority state governments this decade, we must
examine the less-visible features of voting that do not treat all citizens
equally, or technicalities that benefit Republicans or GOP rule. These
are especially important in close races when public enthusiasm is wan-
ing because they decisively affect voting blocs.

No matter which verb you pick—biasing, tilting, gaming, rigging—
the outcome in many races is unfairly handicapped before the votes are
cast. This is why a Democratic president could be reelected in 2012
with 5 million more popular votes, and 1.4 million more Democrats
than Republicans voted for House candidates nationwide, yet the GOP
emerged with 33 more House seats.[53] That same "red shift" persisted
in November 2016, when Clinton won 2.9 million more popular votes
than Trump, but the GOP won a forty-seven-seat US House majority[54]
and ended up with full control of thirty-two state legislatures.[55]

What Democrats did to Bernie and progressives was bad. But
compared to what the GOP has done to all voters this past decade, it
was child's play. There is little on the Democratic side of the aisle that
compares to what Republicans have done on a national scale to build

a structural advantage into winning key state legislatures and House races. The GOP crafted a pre-Election Day advantage that boosts their starting-line odds of winning. Beyond that baseline, the party has been pushing and passing scores of state laws that further erode Democratic voting blocs at key steps in the voting process. In state after state, they have ruthlessly targeted the same voters Democrats are seeking through its registration drives and get-out-the-vote efforts—nonwhites, students, and the poor. The GOP's motives are clear: hold onto power and protect its shrinking and aging white base. (In 1992, nonwhites were 13 percent of the national electorate. In 2016, it was nearly a third.)

Remarkably, the most impactful Republican action to restructure the electoral landscape flew below the national media's radar and was ignored by Democrats until recently—years after it began. Data analysts, however, say that by 2016, the GOP had created upwards of a 6–8 percent[56] built-in lead for many of its candidates for state legislatures and the House. How did they do that? They saw and seized an old but audacious way to resegregate each party's most reliable voters. These are voters who turn out for local, state, and congressional races—not just presidential elections. Republicans identified each party's reliable voters in enough key states, and drew election district lines where more Republicans were likely to show up and vote than Democrats. Because they saturated these districts with their voters and diluted the Democratic base, Republicans could much more easily reach winning majorities.

"The Democrats fell asleep at the switch," said David Daley, author of *Ratf**ked: The True Story Behind The Secret Plan to Steal America's Democracy*,[57] which details how a small team of Republicans foresaw, plotted, and created that advantage after losing nationally in 2008. "They [Democrats] did not pay attention to it. They did not pay attention to it even after Karl Rove laid out the playbook in the *Wall Street Journal* [in March 2010]. They didn't have the strategic imagination to come up with a plan or even the tactical ability to play defense once

Karl Rove spelled it out on the op-ed page of the country's largest newspaper. That's bad. And they have paid the consequences for that this entire decade."[58]

The Republicans assembled majorities by concentrating as many Democrats as they could in few urban districts while spreading out the rest in seats where they would not reach winning majorities. They did that by drilling down and literally choosing which neighborhoods were included in state legislative and House districts. These are not statewide races, such as for governor or US senator or president. These are the jigsaw-puzzle shape districts that elect state legislators and House members. A handful of astute, well-organized Republicans sensed this opportunity in 2009. They realized whichever party held majority power in state legislatures after the 2010 election[59] would redraw political boundaries lasting for the next decade, as most redistricting follows the once-a-decade US census (which recurs in 2020).

The GOP did not have to draw lines that followed logical demarcations like county lines, school districts, or population centers. They forged enough bizarrely shaped districts with a predictably higher Republican turnout to win state legislative majorities and keep the US House red. As Richard Wolf, one of the few national reporters who follows redistricting wrote for *USA Today*, the results were seen immediately. "In 2012, Republicans won 53 percent of the vote but 72 percent of the House seats in [twenty] states where they drew the lines."[60]

This is called gerrymandering—or extreme redistricting. It's wonky, little understood, and underappreciated. But everyone has seen its impact. Think of 2016's presidential results. In Pennsylvania, Trump won statewide by forty-four thousand votes. In Wisconsin, it was by twenty-three thousand votes. In Michigan, it was by eleven thousand votes. In these states, the presidential result—the statewide vote—was split nearly 50–50. That reveals these states are evenly divided before cracking them into smaller pieces. Yet, in these and other purple states this decade, the GOP has routinely won two-thirds or more of state legislative and House seats. How can that be?

The answer is their political maps. There are some instances of Democrats doing this to Republicans—such as a 2011 Maryland ploy to oust a ten-term, Republican congressman (which both parties have litigated and the Supreme Court may hear in 2018). But these are not part of a national Democratic strategy. What Democrats and their allies have typically done in cycle after cycle is register voters, do polling that shapes political advertising and get-out-the-vote (GOTV) efforts, and hope this will coalesce. The Republicans are more aggressive and cynical. They register voters, do analytics, messaging and GOTV, but they don't stop there. They want more certainty and a proven baseline. Redistricting gives them that edge.

8

CREATING PARTISAN GHETTOS

This decade's Republican strategy starts with extreme redistricting: deciding beforehand which electoral races each party's base will vote in. Redistricting is not the elephant in the living room, that is to say, a large and unacknowledged presence we don't want to talk about. Redistricting *is* the living room. It is the field and stage upon which everything else follows.

Redistricting is the biggest verifiable way Republicans have gamed and added points for their side in state and federal elections before candidates are known and voters chime in. That is not all they have done. They keep hyping virtually nonexistent voter impersonation fraud to justify new state-based anti-voter laws such as stricter ID requirements in order to get a ballot at polling places, which nonpartisan analysts such as the US Government Accountability Office found shaves another 2–3 percentage points off the November turnout.[61] Other GOP tactics that reduce turnout include partisan purges of voter lists, limiting early voting, barring same-day registration and voting, and restricting voting by mail.[62] But those suppressive tactics come later, long after extreme redistricting sets the stage.

Extreme is the key word here. Republicans have not abided

by what the federal courts have long said should be the standard. It is not even close. A half century ago, at the height of the civil rights struggle in 1962, the Supreme Court issued a ruling, *Baker v. Carr*, which articulated the ideal of one person one vote when drawing political districts.[63] In 2004, in one of its last decisions before Republicans seized this process in 2011, the court urged partisans to behave. "The orderly working of our Republic, and the democratic process, depends on a sense of decorum and restraint in all branches of government, and in the citizenry itself," wrote Justice Anthony Kennedy for the majority in *Vieth v. Jubelirer*.[64] What the GOP did seven years later, however—where the cases and maps coming before federal courts today originated—showed no restraint or decorum. It was the rawest of power plays, where they saw and executed a ruthless strategy to win.

Daley's book, *Ratf**ked: The True Story Behind The Secret Plan to Steal America's Democracy*, describes what unfolded in excruciating and brilliant detail.[65] A small team, starting with a handful of political junkie consultants, envisioned and executed a two-part plan. Much like the way Democrats felt after 2016's pounding, most Republicans concluded they were headed for political exile after Obama's 2008 landslide victory and the Democrats' sweep of Congress. But a respected Republican political consultant who specialized in tracking state-based campaigns, Chris Jankowski, saw a path back into power.

Jankowski knew the president's party almost always loses seats in midterm elections, the non-presidential years. Moreover, as you go down the ballot to statehouse races, he knew most people voted on party lines because they do not know the candidates. The GOP team he led, known as REDMAP, for REDistricting MAjority Project, looked at the country. It concluded that if Republican candidates won slightly more than one hundred state legislative races in key states like Ohio, Pennsylvania, Wisconsin, and Michigan, and a few governors' races in 2010, that nothing could stop them from a virtually unassailable national comeback.

First, they had to win enough state races to get majorities in the legislative chambers that would redraw maps after the 2010 census. They identified 107 local races in sixteen states that accounted for 190 US House seats and jumped in. REDMAP launched some of the most vicious attacks seen in years in these states. These were radio and TV ads, or mailers landing ten days before 2010's Election Day, when it was too late to respond with media buys. Democratic incumbent women were compared to prostitutes. Longtime incumbents who governed by making compromises were called the worst sellouts. Republicans won twenty-one state legislative chambers in 2010, enough to take over the redistricting process.

Republicans kept their eye on the prize. What does this process look like? Imagine sitting with consultants in front of a bank of computers in a law office—so all conversations are confidential under attorney-client privileges—or in hotel suites near the Capitol building. You stare at something akin to a Google map you can zoom in and out of. The goal is creating districts with roughly the same number of people when the seats are not statewide, countywide, or citywide. In the same way you drag a mouse to change a driving route following different highways, mapmakers could examine neighborhoods down to every block. Their software had voting histories of residents and other demographic data. Jankowski's team tracked the GOP voters who backed their presidential nominee John McCain in 2008—a year they lost badly—and who voted in state elections. They identified their most reliable voters. In some southern states, they tracked voters by race, assuming most non-whites were Democrats.[66]

Based on that threshold of each party's reliable base, they massaged, moved, or radically reset boundaries for state legislative and House races so turnout by Republicans would almost always defeat Democrats. They packed Democrats into blue epicenters, usually cities. That let the GOP to posture their maps as supporting minority candidates. (The Voting Rights Act of 1965 says that is the only allowable use of race—to create districts where minorities can elect representatives.)

Republicans knew what they were doing. They would never win certain seats, but they intentionally concentrated more Democrats so the nearby districts would be more firmly red. In some states, black Democrats even cut deals with the GOP mapmakers to get winning House seats. Their state parties had spurned them.

The first hint of what was to come for the most of this decade was seen immediately after the 2012 election. Obama was reelected with a nationwide 5 million popular vote majority. That showed that Democrats could win majorities when there are no boundaries inside states. But when it came to the US House, even though Democrats cast 1.4 million more votes nationally, the GOP ended up with thirty-three more seats. Democrats who won House seats often had higher overall percentages than Republican victors, but the GOP took more seats. REDMAP successfully resegregated voters: by race, party, or both. They erased competitive districts. Most of these elections were over before they began.

As is always the case in politics, there are publicly given explanations to deflect the truth. One academic study in 2013 downplayed the impact of redistricting, saying Democrats got clobbered because they lived in cities—pushing the geography, not partisan intervention, explanation. But later studies by other experts, such as Princeton University mathematics professor Samuel Wang, found Democrats lost twenty-two seats in 2012 due to gerrymandering.[67]

Looking at each election this decade, a pattern has emerged and held firm. Republicans keep winning an outsized share of state legislative and US House seats despite the closeness of statewide contests. This continued in 2016. Republicans emerged with forty-seven more US House seats than Democrats. That's nearly 11 percent more, when, nationwide, 1.1 percent more GOP votes were cast in House elections. In states targeted by REDMAP—where Trump and Clinton ran neck and neck—the results are stunning. Pennsylvania's US House delegation is 13–5 red to blue. Ohio's is 12–4. Michigan's is 9–5. Virginia's is 7–4. North Carolina's is 10–3. Florida's is 16–11. A May 2017 report by the Brennan Center for Justice at NYU Law School concluded, "extreme partisan bias in congressional maps account for at least 16–17 Republican seats in the current Congress—a significant portion of the 24 seats Democrats would need to gain control of the House."[68]

As bad as the congressional picture is, it's worse in the state legislatures. Since World War II, the president's party has typically lost 450 legislative seats as voter sentiment swings in the opposite direction during his term.[69] Under Obama, Democrats have lost nearly one thousand seats. Daley writes the post-2010 redistricting is "the story of how Republicans turned a looming demographic disaster [its aging shrinking white base] into legislative majorities so unbreakable, so impregnable, that none of the outcomes are in doubt until after the 2020 Census." His book came out before the 2016 election.

"State legislative numbers have not budged over the course of this decade," he said in 2017. "The Ohio House is 66–33 Republican. Pennsylvania is 121–82 Republican. Michigan is 63–47. But what's really interesting to note is that it hasn't budged in those states in 2012, 2014, 2016. It's pretty much [at] the exact same place. They have taken all of the swing districts out of these states and Democrats have not been able to make even the slightest incremental gains in the most important states over this decade—to which I'd add North Carolina, Virginia, Wisconsin, and Florida."

How big a built-in lead do Republicans have? "It takes 55 to 56 percent of the popular vote [of reliable Democrats voting] to have a 50–50 chance" of winning, he said, adding that was an average and in some states it was higher. Other analysts like FiveThirtyEight.com's Harry Enten said the GOP starting line advantage is closer to 8 percent.[70] "The mapmakers know the voters who turn out," Daley said. "These districts are drawn by people with all that information preloaded into their software. They draw lines knowing who turns out and knowing what kind of elections they turn out for."

Other attempts to measure the impact of redistricting agree with these figures. A major development since Daley's book is that federal courts have been looking at a wave of new redistricting lawsuits for the first time in years.[71] With the exception of a GOP suit over a US House seat in Maryland, all of the cases have been filed against Republicans and date back to 2011 and REDMAP's handiwork. In a Wisconsin lawsuit that will be heard by the Supreme Court in its fall 2017 term, voting rights advocates are using a relatively new measure called wasted votes, which is expressed as a percentage of voter turnout.[72]

It was developed by Nicholas O. Stephanopoulos, a University of Chicago law professor leading the team that challenged Wisconsin's Republican gerrymander as illegally partisan. It looks at the percentage of one party's votes that aren't needed to win—that are wasted—when voters are packed into districts (or conversely diluted from winning majorities). That gap in Wisconsin was 13.3 percent in 2012 and 9.6 percent in 2014. Stanford University political scientist Simon Jackson issued a 2015 report based on the 2012 and 2014 cycles that found similar gaps of more than 10 percent in Florida, Indiana, Kansas, Michigan, Missouri, North Carolina, New York, Ohio, Rhode Island, Virginia, Wisconsin, and Wyoming. Only two of these states are blue—New York and Rhode Island.[73]

By mid-2017, federal court rulings over 2011's redistricting seemed to be articulating new rules for when gerrymandering was and wasn't unconstitutional.[74] There are two kinds of redistricting cases. The first involves partisan greed: grabbing as many seats as possible via jigsaw puzzle–like districts. That's where the GOP lost in federal court in Wisconsin, the first ruling in a decade to throw out maps for partisan excess. The GOP's appeal of that ruling was accepted by Supreme Court, which has never thrown out political maps citing excessive partisanship.[75]

The second category of redistricting cases involves the illegal use of race when creating districts. Republicans lost on that issue in lower federal court in Texas. In Virginia and Alabama, the Supreme Court told lower courts to go back and use different standards to examine how the GOP targeted voters by race.[76] In May 2017, the Court—voting

5–3 without its newest member, conservative Neil Gorsuch, ruled that North Carolina had illegally used race to create two House districts. They added tens of thousands of black voters to seats where black congressmen were winning—a tactic to bleach surrounding districts and make them more solidly Republican.[77]

Before North Carolina's ruling, the Court was hesitant to separate illegal racial factors from legal partisan actions. The majority rejected the Republican's rhetoric that they were merely looking for McCain voters and were trying to comply with the Voting Rights Act (VRA) to help create black seats.[78] The majority concluded that North Carolina's GOP subverted the VRA because it first sorted voters by race, not party, and packed thousands into House districts where blacks were already winning. Dissenting justices said North Carolina's GOP didn't use race that way, accused the majority of looking for a "smoking gun," and declared they had no problem with partisan redistricting "while some might find it distasteful."[79]

Remarkably, the majority's opinion also quantified the advantage that extreme redistricting brought North Carolina's Republicans. It noted the GOP has consistently won House races with 56 percent of the vote this decade. In contrast, North Carolina's three Democratic House members were reelected in 2016 with 67 to 69 percent of the vote. This disparity comes from "cracking" and "packing" voters, the slang used by political consultants. In June 2017, the Supreme Court affirmed a lower court ruling that found North Carolina's GOP also had racially gerrymandered twenty-eight state legislative districts. What happens next in the state, as well as in other states where federal courts have ruled against Republicans, is an open question. That is because GOP-run legislatures that have redrawn maps have been accused by Democrats of doing too little to restore balances. That's been the case in Georgia,[80] Alabama,[81] and Texas.[82]

The REDMAP plan didn't just seal a House majority for this decade. It also locked up state legislatures. This structural advantage has fueled ensuing red state rollbacks against voting rights, collective bargaining and union dues, women's reproductive rights, and LGBT rights. It's what has enabled red states' lawsuits against Obamacare, affirmative action in higher education, and challenges to Obama's climate change–related actions. Democrats in 2017 are saying they will never allow a REDMAP-like project to recur. They say the courts are siding with them and ordering red-run states to revise state and congressional districts before 2018. They are focusing on key legislative and gubernatorial races in 2017 and 2018. They say they will have a place at 2021's redistricting and mapmaking tables—with Democratic governors to veto bad maps. We will see.[83]

Beyond the audaciousness and longtime thinking that Republicans saw and imposed on a nation with more Democratic voters, REDMAP underscores how the GOP view elections. They see a system and rules that can be bent to serve their party before all other concerns. April 2017's vote by the Senate's GOP majority to revoke the filibuster rule for Supreme Court confirmations is another example of this pattern. Until then, sixty votes—a bipartisan coalition—were needed to end debate and move to a Senate vote. Majority Leader Mitch McConnell did everything to game the rules to get a right-wing court majority. The GOP blocked Obama's nominee and changed the filibuster rule to seat Gorsuch. They put their party before country, played dirty, and won.

Democrats typically take more fair-minded approaches, such as expanding the electorate. They are generally more naive and less cynical, less ruthless. They express those values with voter registration drives in underrepresented communities, by filing lawsuits to uphold voting rights, and by trying to prompt new voters to turn out—especially the young and nonwhites. That's wide-eyed compared to the surgical thinking executed by Jankowski and REDMAP. Targeting reliable proven voters is more concrete. Republicans do not solely rely on enlarging their base and getting out that vote.

It's taken me a while to see this. I first heard the left's registration boasts in Ohio in 2004, when EMILY's List, the PAC for women candidates, said they helped register hundreds of thousands of voters.

They did not know or appreciate that Ohio's hyper-partisan secretary of state, Republican J. Kenneth Blackwell, had overseen purges of large numbers of voters in the bluest cities. (From 2011–2016 under his GOP successor, Ohio has purged 2 million voters, more than any other state.[84]) That tactic was one of many that Blackwell used to undermine Democrats. EMILY's List had perfectly good intentions. But they did not realize how far behind they were to start. They were optimistic they could get new voters to cast ballots. The Republican calculus was more precise and cutthroat. Jankowski's tactics were an expression of his party's do-everything-to-win philosophy.

No other voter suppression tactic scales with the impact of extreme redistricting. The GOP wants their voters to turn out and they work at it. They don't mind if Democrats turn out as long as that's in districts Democrats were going to win anyway—and the GOP controls the levers of state power and the US House. What's revealing about the 2011 gerrymander is it's the one strategy they are least likely to brag about—notwithstanding Rove's *Wall Street Journal* op-ed in March 2010. Compared to their rants about voter fraud and Democrats cheating, it is all but invisible. That affirms how significant it is.

In politics, insiders who know what's going on have an unspoken code of silence. The rarest commodity in politics is trust. It's only recently—mostly since Daley's book in mid-2016—that REDMAP's architects are telling their story. Other GOP mapmakers have kept mum. Some have been sued in states like Florida, where they recruited people to submit maps to supposedly nonpartisan state redistricting commissions. A quarter of the states have these panels. These consultants are playing dumb in court by discounting the power and impact of gerrymandering. (They may not have to do that after the Supreme Court's North Carolina ruling, where its conservatives said there was nothing illegal about partisan power grabs—the issue in the Wisconsin case.[85])

While extreme redistricting is emerging from the shadows as 2018 and 2020 loom, we need to turn to other antidemocratic features the

GOP has placed atop this foundation. But it is critical to hold onto the view that the playing field is not level at its starting line. It is not even close. The goddess of liberty is not holding one scale in each hand, awaiting voters to weigh in equally. Aided by no serious opposition from Democrats in 2010, Republicans segregated voters to regain power. They built a 6 to 8 percent starting-line head start for scores of state and federal contests. However, even that advantage wasn't enough.

"The pattern is really, really clear. The first thing gerrymandered legislatures do in most of these states is try and limit voting rights. The second thing they do is go after labor rights. The third thing is women's rights," Daley said. "There is a deep connection. It makes it much easier to win closer statewide races when you can limit the Democratic turnout and minority turnout with new voter ID laws, by making it harder to register, by conducting purges of voting rolls, by eliminating early voting days, all that."

9

LOOKING FORWARD, NOT BACKWARD

SOME OF THE MOST CONSEQUENTIAL TRENDS in elections arrive with little fanfare. That was the case with the GOP's extreme 2011 gerrymander. The same is true with their next serious attack: suppressing major Democratic voting blocs. Unlike the twentieth-century's civil rights movement where the most visible bad guys were local police using clubs and fire hoses, this century's bad guys are a Brooks Brothers Riot of briefcase-carrying lawyers armed with shrill testimony and partisan propaganda. But they seek the same result: to keep the electorate from growing and diversifying by complicating the process and restricting who gets to vote.

A dozen years ago, I witnessed a moment marking the arrival of Republican's fabricated crusade against what they call voter fraud. I remember thinking this cannot be serious. It was after 2004's presidential election in Ohio, where Republicans vehemently went after Democratic voters. A little-known lawyer showed up at a poorly attended congressional field hearing to offer the GOP's counternarrative: cheating Democrats were the problem that needed fixing. Partisan accusations have been around forever. But his tirade had no basis. Hordes of imposters inundating the polls? Voting for Democrats but not getting caught? And all of this in red-run states such as Ohio?

This scenario was right out of nineteenth-century America. Then, urban machines and rural bosses paid so-called "repeaters" to do just this, as the University of Kentucky's Tracy Campbell describes in his 2005 book, *Deliver The Vote: A History of Election Fraud as an American Political Tradition—1742–2004.*[86] A century ago, little was akin to today's statewide registration rolls, polling place voter lists, and check-in protocols. If you sign in to get a ballot with a fake name today, you are signing a perjury confession. That's a serious crime, ticket to a large fine, and possibly jail.

This is not to say that individuals do not make mistakes or try to game the system. Every election sees a handful of ex-felons who have not regained their voting rights trying to cast a ballot. There are a handful of people who think they can vote in more than one state as long as they own property there. There also are a few people who try to impersonate another voter—the textbook GOP definition of voter fraud. They typically are a candidate's relative or a local official seeking reelection.[87] Those are real-world examples. But these incidents literally are once-in-a-million voter occurrences, infinitesimal exceptions in a nation where multimillions routinely vote. They are so rare, so inconsequential, compared to real margins swinging elections, that something else is going on. And indeed there is.

Republicans know they cannot hold onto power when their base is aging and shrinking compared to the rest of the country's demographics. So they have seized upon a prejudice-fueled strategy as an excuse to overly police the process in pursuit of a phantom menace: Illegal Democratic voters. Despite producing no evidence that this is a real problem of any magnitude, combating voter fraud has become the GOP's go-to excuse this century to pass scores of state laws that complicate voting for entire populations trending blue. Those laws peel off slices of Democratic voters—percent by percent. Every year, hundreds of thousands of ballots are spoiled, misread, or disqualified across the country.[88] Yet Republicans don't ever complain about that—or make federal cases over it.

Nonetheless, because the voter fraud meme draws on partisan vitriol, serves a partisan purpose, and crucially—there is no federal agency that definitively tracks it[89]—the GOP has been using it to pass a spectrum of state laws and rules to intentionally disrupt voting.[90] The GOP persists despite investigations by the Department of Justice, federal courts, Congress, academics, and journalists, some of whom have noted real-world instances of illegal voting are literally rarer than getting hit by lightning.[91] Another confirmation came in April 2017 in a federal court ruling that threw out a Texas 2011 voter ID law as racially discriminatory against blacks and Latinos. The ruling noted that Texas had "two convictions for in-person voter impersonation fraud out of 20 million votes in the decade leading up to SB 14's [the law's] passage."[92]

Numbers like that are not unusual. After the incumbent GOP governor of North Carolina, Pat McCrory, narrowly lost his 2016 reelection bid, his campaign consultants challenged the results by saying six hundred people fraudulently voted. They hastily fabricated and filed legal papers that named innocent people who were smeared in the local press. It was a ruse to try to throw the governor's race to its legislature, where Republicans held the majority. The State Board of Elections' April 2017 report found only two people impersonated another voter in 2016—"family members voting in place of a recently deceased loved one."[93] That was out of 4.6 million votes cast.

The right-wing Heritage Foundation's post-2016 report of all national examples of false registrations, ineligible voting, fraudulent use of absentee ballots, and duplicate voting cites 492 cases and 733 convictions from 1982 through 2016.[94] That is one case for every 2 million presidential election voters from 1984 to 2016 (approximately 980 million votes were cast).[95] If you count by convictions, where some people pleaded to more than one charge, that total was still less than one in a million voters. Although there were more elections in America and multimillions more people voting in this period, which further dilutes their figures, Heritage nonetheless uses its report to further police the polls.

But made-up menaces serve a purpose. Republicans know it doesn't matter if they are pilloried in the press as long as they manipulate the rules of voting and elections. They don't care if political gain means disadvantaging opponents, including racially hostile tactics and openly discriminatory results. Looking back, I was present when a messenger arrived to herald the return of this phantom menace and its sleazy rationale. It was more layered and consequential than I realized at the time. But not taking this ruse seriously is exactly how Republicans finesse restrictions on voting into law and elections.

The confrontation pitted some of the civil rights movement's heroines—women born under segregation who became members of Congress—against this century's voting suppressors. Like Karl Rove's *Wall Street Journal* op-ed on REDMAP's strategy, it heralded a national wave of anti-voting tactics that continues today. Trump's Commission on Election Integrity, announced in spring 2017, is being cochaired by, and has seated people, whose attacks on nonwhite voters began during this time. Since he took office, more states have passed anti-voter laws than during the Obama Administration's final two years. The rationale was countering the made-up menace of voter fraud.[96]

The setting in 2004 was a city auditorium in Columbus, Ohio. The Committee on House Administration, which oversees elections, was holding a hearing blandly entitled, *2004 Election and the Implementation of The Help America Vote Act*.[97] That law provided several billion dollars to states to buy new electronic voting machines as the response to Florida's problem-plagued presidential election in 2000. The hearing's title papered over two competing agendas. The committee's Republican chairman, Ohio's Bob Ney, wanted to place a whitewashed version of what happened in Ohio into the record. Weeks before, the House Judiciary Committee's Democrats had other ideas and took testimony detailing partisan barriers that delayed and disenfranchised tens of thousands of voters.

Seated besides Ney were two now-deceased black Democratic congresswomen. Stephanie Tubbs-Jones, Ohio's first black congresswoman, was an ex-judge and local prosecutor from Cleveland. Six weeks before she stood in the US Capitol building with California Democratic Sen. Barbara Boxer to challenge the ratification of the 2004 Electoral College vote. They forced the House and Senate to return to their chambers and hear complaints about GOP-led voter suppression for two hours. Juanita Millender-McDonald was a PhD educator representing Los Angeles who grew up in Alabama. They came to question Republicans such as Ohio Secretary of State Kenneth Blackwell, who refused to shake Tubbs-Jones' hand and then bragged about that as a witness. Bleackwell is at the time of this writing on Trump's election integrity commission.

State Senate President Jeff Jacobson testified he didn't understand why Ohio had become a poster child of problem voting. Without blinking, Millender-McDonald asked about one notorious tactic. Why had Blackwell's office told county officials to reject registrations that weren't printed on 80-pound paper—a heavier stock than copied forms used by grassroots groups? Jacobson's surreal reply hinted at the GOP's arguments to come, and not just in Ohio—but on Fox News for years.

"I would just say that fraudulent registrations are not part of the American way and groups that are paid to come in and end up registering Mickey Mouse and some of the other people that were registered in return for crack cocaine, the millions of dollars that poured in, in an attempt to influence Ohio, I think, is not normal and I would just state that it did make all of our jobs quite a bit more difficult," Jacobson said, justifying efforts to reject registrations turned in by civil rights groups like the NAACP or antipoverty groups like ACORN, the Association of Community Organizers for Reform Now.[98]

Millender-McDonald was as dignified as the state senator was unbound.

"Mr. Jacobson, I would hate for you to characterize voters as crack cocaine," she began, carefully choosing her words. "Please do not characterize those who are doing the registration of people—"

"You may not be aware of what specifically happened," he interrupted. "A gentleman was arrested and I think pled guilty that he was paid in crack cocaine for submitting registration cards and the registration cards that he submitted included Donald Duck, Mickey Mouse, Mary Poppins, and all kinds of others."

"Of course we have heard that, but is that not one incident of the many?" she said. "We have to be very careful that we do not show any semblance of arrogance on the parts of those who wish to vote and let their vote be counted. There are many minorities in this state and in every state who have been at the throws of not letting their votes be counted."

That exchange showed one party giving voters the benefit of the doubt and the other party doubting voters. It pitted the lessons from last century's voting rights movement against this century's vote suppressors. Despite his bluntness, Jacobson signaled the start of the GOP argument and strategy: seize on singular incidents of malfeasance— such as a registration group's bad hire who forged voter applications, which is easily caught and prosecuted. Then hype that lone example into a menace to justify new laws that intentionally complicate voting for entire statewide populations, but especially targeting Democrats.

Millender-McDonald urged him not to respond disproportionately—but that was what the Republicans in Ohio and nationwide intended to do. Later that afternoon as she left for the airport, the most important witness testified and submitted a written report. Mark 'Thor' Hearne cut his remarks short because of the hour. He was a Missouri lawyer who worked with Rove on Bush's 2004 campaign. No Democrat there knew him. Nor had anyone heard of the American Center for Voting Rights he represented. Its website was launched only a few days before. As the Democrats focused on the election that barely ended, Hearne and the GOP looked to the future. He had come to launch a new wave of voter suppression.

"Reprehensible acts" marred the 2004 election, Hearne said, such as the submission of fake registration forms by left-leaning groups associated with the Democrats. He spoke of "an onslaught made against the Ohio election system," including lawsuits from civil rights groups that "caused great chaos and confusion and difficulty for the election officials seeking to implement Ohio law and made it more difficult to have a fair and honest election." His prepared remarks, which he submitted after condensing them, were more pointed. "Voter fraud was reported in every corner of the state and fraudulent voter registrations totaled in the thousands," his script said. "Ohio citizens deserve the confidence that they—the voters—not trial lawyers, activist judges and special interest groups soliciting voters with crack cocaine determine the result of Ohio elections."[99]

Hearne also submitted a report for the Congressional Record, which Ney accepted. It was a declaration of political war. Hearne and its coauthors, all Republican lawyers, went after every major Democratic political committee, voting rights organization, labor union, and antipoverty group. It cites "MoveOn operatives," polls "stalked by ACLU and 'voter rights' operatives," and even a "table operated by MoveOn that promised 'Free Coffee.'" These examples were beyond shrill, but they served a partisan point. Everyone Hearne cited not only supported expanding voting rights, but was a coconspirator in a vast conspiracy—a characterization that endures today as Republicans keep pounding the voter fraud drum.[100]

Hearne's report did cite one-off mistakes by people working for registration groups like ACORN—who, as noted in the Heritage Foundation's 2016 report, were quickly caught by authorities. Every election has human errors, hubris, and passionate excess. But in a state with 5.7 million presidential voters in 2004, there is a false equivalency between isolated events where no illegal votes resulted, and statewide remedies complicating the process or preventing tens of thousands of voters. As Millender-McDonald warned, what matters is separating the one from the many.

Neither Hearne nor any Republicans at that hearing cared about twenty-six thousand Ohioans whose regular ballots were not counted, nor about thirty thousand Ohioans given provisional ballots that were later disqualified, nor about tens of thousands who waited hours in the rain because polls in Democratic cities didn't have enough voting machines.[101] Instead, they signaled the GOP would soon revive its pursuit of voter fraud with the White House fully behind it.

As Michael Waldman put it in his book, *The Fight To Vote*, Republicans were chasing the one problem that did not exist. But they chased it. Two years later, after three hundred investigations by the Justice Department, 119 people had been charged with voter fraud nationwide, with eighty-six convictions. One was a Wisconsin ex-felon who voted before his voting rights had been restored. In West Virginia, a sheriff, police chief, and a court clerk were caught paying residents $20 to vote for a slate of local candidates.[102] This is truly small-time stuff. That record, nonetheless, prompted Bush's Attorney General, Alberto Gonzales, to fire seven federal prosecutors—which caused a scandal eventually leading to resignations by Gonzales and Rove, then a senior White House strategist.[103]

The voter fraud meme did not stop there. It solidified into a doctrinaire Republican belief that Democrats steal elections—when, if anything, it is the Republicans who are guilty of this crime in the early twenty-first century. As the 2008 presidential race closed, GOP nominee John McCain accused ACORN of "perpetuating massive voter fraud," even though there was no proof. After Democrats won the White House and Congress that year, REDMAP emerged.[104] The GOP won key statehouse majorities in November 2010, but Republicans did not only set their sights on redrawing districts. Many believed McCain's finger-pointing. Fox News and Breitbart.com kept the hysteria alive. They now had majorities to solidify Republican advantages by rewriting more rules for voting.

The first thing Republicans did after their extreme redistricting was go after voting rights. In legislative sessions starting in January 2011, GOP voter suppression moved forward big time. Backed by front groups and right-wing legislation mills like the American Legislative

Exchange Council, GOP legislators introduced more than 180 bills in forty-one states to toughen voter ID laws, cut back early voting, and penalize registration drive errors.[105] The argument—made by some of the same people now on Trump's "election integrity" commission—was to combat voter fraud. Rhetoric aside, it was a war over access to the ballot.

10

THE VOTING WARS

It's an open question if Republicans outside of elite circles like REDMAP knew how effective their 2011 gerrymander would be—locking up state legislatures and House majorities for every election cycle this decade. But party leaders knew measures like tougher photo ID requirements to get a ballot at precincts would cut into Democratic turnout. Royal Masset, the Texas Republican Party political director, told the *Houston Chronicle* in 2007 that stricter ID laws could "add 3 percent to the Republican vote."[106]

A 2014 study by the congressional nonpartisan Government Accountability Office on tougher voter ID laws in Kansas and Tennessee found that Masset was not far off. Those laws reduced turnout in Kansas by 1.9 percent and in Tennessee 2.2 percent, the GAO said.[107] A May 2017 study by Demos, a think tank headed by former Connecticut secretary of state, Miles Rapoport, a Democrat, found that stricter ID laws in Wisconsin, Virginia, and Mississippi caused turnout to drop by an average of 1.7 percent statewide. However, "turnout in counties with a high black population" was 2.8 percent lower.[108]

Other research parses the impact of strict voter ID laws on non-whites even further. Three academics analyzing 2006–2014 data from the Cooperative Congressional Election Study, which sampled over a third of a million voters, found starker numbers. Compared to less

restrictive states, stricter ID states—such as Texas, Florida, Arizona—
saw November black turnout fall by 2.1 percent, Asian turnout fall by
5.0 percent, and Latino turnout fall by 8.3 percent. The drop-off was
even larger in primary elections. "By instituting strict voter ID laws,
states can alter the electorate and shift outcomes toward those on the
right," coauthors Zoltan L. Hajnal of the University of California San
Diego, Nazita Lajevardi of Michigan State University, and Lindsay
Neilson of Bucknell University wrote for the *Washington Post* in
February 2017.[109]

What's happened to the electoral landscape for the past decade
has been nothing less than an ongoing war of attrition. The pendulum
first swings to the right after red states pass laws to make it harder
for Democratic voting blocs to participate. That's been followed by a
push back in court by civil rights groups seeking to restore procedural
and voting options, where some of the partisan advantages favoring
Republicans are undone. In states where voting wars have been most
intense, voters, poll workers, and election officials have been left confused by last-minute court rulings and administrative directives. That's
not an accident. Complicating the process also discourages participation, and lower-turnout elections favor the GOP's base. This dynamic
is not just seen in presidential swing states. States that could put the
House in play—or should be a swing state like Georgia—have watched
Republicans postpone what should be their relegation to history
books—if demography was destiny.

More than one voting rights attorney has referred to the teens
as a lost decade. What followed 2010's electoral GOP victories and
redistricting was a pattern that has been repeated in each two-year
cycle since. Soon after new legislatures convene—typically January
in odd-numbered years—numerous red states saw dozens of bills
introduced to make voting more onerous for those states' Democrats.
Republicans almost never propose anything that affects voting by
mail—absentee ballots—which their wealthier suburban base prefers.
It is almost all aimed at polling places and precinct-based voting, which

many urban voters prefer and where first-time voters are required to cast their ballot.

Some of the most aggressive voter suppression bills were rushed through legislatures without hearings and were quickly signed into law. This started in 2011, when scores of bills were introduced in forty-one states.[110] In nineteen states, twenty-five bills became law along with gubernatorial executive orders. These included tougher voter ID requirements, such as Texas barring state university photo IDs but allowing state handgun licenses. Wisconsin also created a photo ID requirement that excluded university IDs. Florida adopted big fines for voter registration drive errors, which stopped the League of Women Voters' effort for the 2012 presidential election. Ohio ended early voting on the last Sunday before Election Day, when clergy led congregations in a "souls to the polls" push. States scheduled voter purges in Democratic strongholds shortly before the presidential election. Kansas added a proof of citizenship requirement to its state registration form and passed a tougher ID law. Both measures discouraged nonwhites and youths from voting in state elections. All were aimed at Democrats.

Against this array of barriers came a rapid response by civil rights groups and Obama's Department of Justice. Many laws were challenged in state and federal courts. The DOJ came in under the Voting Rights Act of 1965.[111] That law, a high watermark of the Civil Rights Movement, requires the Justice Department to approve any change in voting laws or rules in states and counties with histories of racial discrimination in elections. It applied almost completely to the Old South, however, and not states such as Wisconsin, which have led Republican voter suppression efforts this decade. Nonetheless, under its so-called preclearance provision, the DOJ could veto anything it found would discriminate against minorities, compared to that jurisdiction's current rules.

The ensuing court fights did not correspond neatly to the election cycles. Many started in one and continued into the next. In some cases, new laws were put on hold while lawsuits unfolded. In other instances they were not. When the spate of new anti-voter bills was first introduced in 2011, the Brennan Center estimated the new laws could make it harder for five million people to vote nationally. That became a front page *New York Times* story. But after many legal challenges were filed, the Center reported anti-voter laws in fourteen states "have been blocked, blunted, repealed or postponed" just before the 2012 election.[112]

That red-to-blue swing of the pendulum faced an abrupt reversal in 2013 that endures today. In a lawsuit and ruling that voting rights activists long feared, a right-wing Supreme Court majority ruled that preclearance—VRA's Section 5—was unconstitutional. Chief Justice John Roberts wrote race relations had evolved so the DOJ's oversight was obsolete.[113] In a flash, states and counties with histories of discrimination in voting were deregulated. States under Section 5 jurisdiction in 2013 were Alabama, Alaska, Arizona, Georgia, Louisiana, Mississippi, South Carolina, Texas, and Virginia. Preclearance also covered counties and cities in California, Florida, New York, North Carolina, South Dakota, and Michigan.[114]

The lawsuit prompting the ruling came from Shelby County, Alabama. It was designed by right-wing lawyers specifically to challenge the VRA's toughest provision. These advocates also drafted the federal suit challenging affirmative action in state university admissions that made it to the Supreme Court—but lost. These are white supremacists that say civil rights groups are unduly negative and backward by continuing to focus on racial identity, racial differences, and discrimination.[115] Publicly, they feign the nation has moved beyond racial divides. While this was all before Trump's overtly racist 2016 campaign, they were aware what their GOP allies would do—restore race-based voter suppression measures in states where white governing classes are threatened by diversity.[116]

Within hours of the Supreme Court's ruling, states demonstrated the absurdity of Justice John Roberts's opinion. Texas, North Carolina, and Alabama immediately acted to pass or announce they would begin enforcing anti-voter laws that had been stuck in court.[117] Overnight, the voting rights pendulum swung hard to the right. Voter suppression had been legalized anew for the 2014 midterms, 2016 presidential election, and local races—and was embraced in red states.

What's often overlooked in analyses of *Shelby County v. Holder* is how many voting law changes came before the DOJ for their preapproval—and involved local elections, such as those for city councils and university boards. The DOJ website said for the decade before *Shelby* it had "received between 4,500 and 5,500 Section 5 submissions, and had reviewed between 14,000 and 20,000 changes in voting laws and procedures annually.[118] A June 2016 report by the NAACP Legal Defense Fund noted, "More than 85 percent of pre-clearance work previously done under Section 5 was at the local level."[119]

The NAACP report highlighted the most common discriminatory tactics that ensued after the VRA was gutted, all of which dilute turnout or tilt the outcome in close races. These "include reducing the number of polling places; changing or eliminating early voting days and/or hours; replacing district voting with at-large elections [undercutting strong local candidates]; implementing onerous registration requirements like proof of citizenship; and removing qualified voters from registration lists." What the NAACP didn't quantify was what the GAO and Demos documented, and what Texas GOP Chair Royal Masset had said: that tactics like these shave a few points off of voter turnout, especially among Democrats.

By 2017, many voting rights groups have been saying that the pendulum was starting to swing back their way, as growing numbers of state and federal judges had been offended by the Republican's antidemocratic playbook. They note that courts are ordering states to redraw political districts marred by racially motivated gerrymandering, to stop enforcing new voter ID laws, and to reverse other anti-voter measures like cutting early voting. They cite progress that Democrats and their allies have made, such as states instituting more registration options and Oregon's model of universal automatic registration.[120]

That view is accurate but incomplete. What it omits is that in the states that determine federal power—House races and presidential swing states—and states where the political complexion is purple or trending blue, that advocates of expanding voting rights are on the defensive.[121] Also, lower-court victories have been hamstrung by GOP-filed appeals—or by legislators dragging their feet to fix laws, or unfairly doing so, despite losing in court.[122] Meanwhile, voting rights groups face new barriers in these states, as Republicans seeking more restrictive voting keep launching new offensives. The result is an ongoing spectrum of rules and requirements that makes voting anything but easy. The NAACP's post-*Shelby* report described the pinpoint targeting of attacks that led up to and fed into 2016. Each attack seeks to peel away blue voters: A few percent here, a few percent there.

LAYERED AND NUANCED ATTACKS

TAKE THE PURPLE STATE OF VIRGINIA. Consider what's unfolded since *Shelby*. In 2013, after the Supreme Court threw out the DOJ's veto power over local changes, Virginia—which had been under the VRA—did what a lot of red states did. It wasn't the most egregious. Its GOP governor and legislature quickly passed a tougher voter ID requirement. It was to take effect the following year in June 2014. Before *Shelby*, the DOJ would likely have blocked this law. Civil rights groups sued and noted 197,000 Virginians didn't have a state driver's license—an acceptable form of ID. Many were nonwhites and lower-income.[123]

Shrewdly, the ID law's authors added a provision so Virginians could get a free state ID. That was what they cited in court. Virginians had to make an effort, they said. Democracy should not be taken for granted, they argued, and the new law provided such a path. Yet a year later, fewer than five thousand Virginians had gotten that free state ID in order to vote. That result was what Republicans expected. That's how voter suppression works. The federal district judge who tossed

Texas's ID law also noted 608,000 residents lacked ID, whereas the
state issued 279 substitute IDs—showing the same voter suppression
template.[124] Virginia's voter ID law remained in effect for 2016's election and was upheld in court that December.

Virginia's voter ID fight wasn't in a vacuum. It had other voter
suppression battles. After the 2010 election, Republicans aggressively
packed black voters into twelve legislative districts in the Richmond-
Hampton Roads region along its southeastern border. That gerrymander was challenged in court as racially discriminatory, prompting a
federal court to order the state legislature to redraw its maps in early
2016. New maps were created, but that legal fight has continued with
the US Supreme Court telling a lower court to use different standards
in assessing whether the gerrymander was partisan, which is legal,
while racial sorting is not. Both Democrats and Republicans claimed
victory, but contested lines remain in effect.[125]

There's more. In 2013, Virginia's political landscape shifted. That
November, Democrat Terry McAuliffe was elected governor, starting
a four-year term in 2014. Two years later, he signed an executive order
restoring voting rights to two hundred thousand Virginians convicted
of nonviolent felonies who served their sentences and completed pro-
bation or parole. Many were youths caught up in the war on drugs.
The state was one of four in the country that banned ex-felons from
voting for life. Virginia Republicans sued McAuliffe, arguing his
clemency was an abuse of power because it did not look at individual
cases. State courts put the rights restoration on hold. In July 2016, the
Virginia Supreme Court killed it and ordered 11,662 ex-felons who had
registered to vote to be removed from voter rolls. McAuliffe responded
that he would act to individually restore their rights.[126] In early 2017,
McAuliffe reported that he had restored the voting rights of 140,000
people.[127] Virginia's Republicans have yet to respond, but may be waiting until McAuliffe's term ends in January 2018.

These pendulum swings show how layered and deliberate
Republicans are with trying to nullify slivers of the Democrats'

base. It is maddening. State courts uphold a stricter voter ID law that adds complexities to the process for all of a state's voters, but block a governor who restores voting rights to a disadvantaged class. Republicans in Virginia and elsewhere don't care about ex-felons' due process rights. They care about preserving political power. As Marty Connors, then chairman of the Alabama Republican Party, told the *Washington Post* in 2004 when asked about felon re-enfranchisement, "As frank as I can be, we're opposed to [it] because felons don't tend to vote Republican."[128]

Needless to say, the states drawing the hardest lines against felon voting are states where restoring that right would threaten Republican rule. Nationally in 2016, six million ex-felons had lost their voting rights, according to the Brennan Center. A third were black—one-in-thirteen voting-age blacks across the United States, Brennan reported. Half a million are in Texas. A quarter million are in Georgia. But Florida is the worst. There, 1.6 million—one in ten voting-age adults—are disenfranchised for life (although civil rights groups are hoping to put a state constitutional amendment changing that before voters in 2018).[129]

Virginia is a typical state in the voting war of attrition. It's purple and a presidential swing state. It's in the GOP mainstream and has close ties to the national party in Washington. Its tug-of-war on voting rights are indicative of this past decade, where political and legal fights have unfurled in state-by-state silos—even as they use a similar playbook. Unless you live in these states, you are unlikely to hear about these power plays, ongoing court fights, their complexities and often-unresolved nature. Yet, these battles are all preambles to the stage upon which the 2016 election was set, including purple-trending states that saw aggressive anti-voter attacks—such as Georgia and North Carolina.

We'll soon delve into what went on there—because it is part of a landscape that is setting the stage for 2018 and 2020. But first we need to step back to get a better foundation in order to understand what the GOP's hit men are pursuing in the fine print of election law. They are burrowing into deeper parts of the process where federal and state laws can be ambiguous and have not been subject to enough lawsuits for clear national standards to emerge. So far, we have touched on big frames—redistricting, changing the rules to one side's benefit, propaganda about fake threats to facilitate restrictive laws. Now we have to step back.

There's another lens that can clarify where other serious anti-voter attacks are occurring. If we think about voting as a narrative with a beginning, middle, and end, we can pinpoint why what's described as a technicality is anything but. Otherwise, it is easy to get lost in details of state-by-state fights, or get distracted by meaningless digressions from election officials or aggressive partisans.

One irrelevant detail that repeatedly surfaces is the claim that voter rolls are a gold mine for fraudulent behavior, when, in reality, they are not. Think about how many times you have heard a TV news reporter blare that voter rolls include dead people. "People that have died 10 years ago are still voting," Trump said at an October 2016 rally in Green Bay, Wisconsin. Well, dead people do not notify election offices that they have died and ask to be removed. They also don't vote—unless they voted early and passed away before Election Day, which is legal. It's an empty concern.[130]

That illegal voter meme points to a corner of election law that has come under increasing GOP attack: voter registration rolls and how they are kept current. There are protocols about how county officials clean up their rolls, and how they face the same problem with people who die as with people who move—and they're not notified of the change. These steps are in the legal nuts and bolts of the voter registration process. If we want to see how the GOP is playing dirty, and how the same people who have been behind the worst suppression gambits are resurfacing under Trump, we must examine what voter registration is and isn't, as well as voter purges.

11

THE STARTING LINE

To begin to see how a straightforward process such as voter registration can be needlessly twisted, we first turn to Alabama. Its political culture repeatedly elected Jefferson Beauregard Sessions III to positions of power, first as state attorney general and US senator, before being picked by Trump as US Attorney General, where he now sits atop national voting rights enforcement. Sessions' namesake are his father and grandfather, both named after Jefferson Davis, the Confederate's president, and Pierre Gustave Toutant-Beauregard, the general who ordered the attack on Fort Sumter that started the Civil War. As a federal prosecutor in 1985, he tried but failed to convict three Alabama activists for voter fraud after they helped with absentee ballots. One was a former aide to Dr. Martin Luther King Jr.[131] That sounds like long ago, but the past is never far behind the fine print of American elections.

Alabama didn't just pass a stricter voter ID law within days of the *Shelby* decision with redistricting and announcements of intention to enforce it. As 2016's cycle began, the state tried to close thirty-one state motor vehicles offices across Alabama's "Black Belt" counties, where residents could get an approved ID. It backtracked by reopening those offices for one day each month, prompting civil rights groups to sue.[132] Alabama's GOP-led redistricting also has been in federal court for most of this decade, where civil rights groups repeatedly won rulings that its state Senate maps were unconstitutional racial gerrymanders. Instead of appealing for a second time to the US Supreme Court, its Republican-majority legislature adopted new maps in May 2017—on a party-line vote. That prompted black Democrats to cry foul and predict they would be back in court.[133] That fight may leave Alabama's maps in place for 2018, however.

But that's not all. Alabama is among a handful of states where Republicans want to impose a secondary voter registration system to winnow who gets to vote in its state elections. This would not affect voting for Congress and president, but for local and state contests on the same day. This is another strategy for resegregating who gets to vote—atop gerrymandering—and is more than reminiscent of Jim Crow days. As Ari Berman has noted in *The Nation*, the impact of these anti-voter laws in the South is turning Democrats into a party of nonwhites and Republicans into a party of whites.[134]

These states seeking a separate, unequal, and secondary state registration process—Alabama, Arizona, Kansas, and Georgia[135]—updated the voter fraud meme in a way that anticipated Trump's big lie that millions of illegal immigrants voted in 2016, keeping him from a popular victory. These states want people registering to vote to provide paper proof of American citizenship. That's usually a birth certificate, passport, or naturalization papers, which not everyone has and takes time and money to get. As with voter fraud, there's no federal agency that maintains an authoritative US citizenship database.[136]

A handful of powerful Republicans in these states unapologetically keep pushing for this secondary standard despite seeing variations of this ploy lose in federal court. They know their allies in high statewide office can keep throwing the first punch by implementing new voter requirements and then fighting via ensuing litigation. That's because voter registration is done at the state level. The fact there is no authoritative federal database of all citizens creates an ambiguity they knowingly exploit. To understand why this is not just odious but could open a major new frontier for GOP-led voter suppression, we have to parse the starting line of voting in America, the registration process.

Unlike most western countries and Canada, voter registration is not automatic for all adult citizens. Most people know they have to register, and if the state doesn't offer it online then federal registration forms are available at the post office. The exceptions are North Dakota, the only state that doesn't require any voter registration, and Oregon, which in 2016 became the first state to automatically enroll everyone who was getting a driver's license. (A half dozen other blue states have taken steps to follow Oregon's example.)

At first glance, registration seems simple. To be an eligible voter, you must be a citizen, a state resident, and at least eighteen years old. That's cited in most state Constitutions. Additional requirements often include not being a convicted felon (most states), not judged mentally incompetent, and swearing to uphold the state and federal constitutions.[137] The federal voter application form seeks this basic information, which is then copied by election office workers from paper forms into computerized voter databases. The data fields or categories are clear: one's first, middle, and last name; street address, city, county, and state; political party if you're joining one; and an identifying ID— usually a state driver's license or the federal Social Security number.[138] Registrants also sign their name, which provides a signature (and signature image) and crucially constitutes a legal oath under penalty of perjury—a major offense.

From this baseline, officials who run elections—usually at the county level—will ensure you get the right ballot with party primaries and correct local and regional races. They will add you to polling place lists (if you are not voting by mail). This is straightforward until snafus emerge with partisan overtones—such as removing infrequent voters from rolls, or moving local polling places without telling voters. But those come later. States also ask people that apply for a driver's license if they want to register, under the National Voter Registration Act of 1993 (also called the motor voter law). The NVRA requires military recruiters and other state agencies to offer registration. But many states have not done so at their welfare offices—prompting lawsuits. (The NVRA also specifies how state officials are to conduct voter list purges, to protect voters but to remove people who move or die.)

Some constraints appear at this electoral starting line. The first, imposed by states and parties, are registration deadlines. These recur before every election, including possibly the upcoming one if you are a new voter. In 2016, only thirteen states and Washington, DC, had Election Day registration, which allowed any eligible person to show up, register, and vote.[139] Two more states, Ohio and Maryland, allow people who come to early-voting centers to do all this. The rest have deadlines lasting from several days to a month before. Some states, like New York, have longer deadlines for party primaries. No one who had not registered six months prior could vote in its 2016's presidential primary.

Then there are requirements that have nothing to do with one's legal eligibility to vote. This is where a simple process gets murky. The most obvious is requiring a specific state-issued photo ID to get a ballot. No state constitution says a plastic card is a requirement to be an eligible voter. But come Election Day, there it is in seventeen states, especially in red states.[140] One exception had been Arkansas, where its Supreme Court in 2014 overturned a GOP-sponsored ID law. The Court said that was an unconstitutional "additional qualification" and compared it to the state's segregation-era poll tax. In March 2017, however, the Republican Gov. Asa Hutchinson signed a bill reinstating the photo ID law. He claimed that new legislation was different and would withstand legal scrutiny.[141]

But the constraint that is likely to assume a higher profile under Trump is the paper proof of citizenship to register. That's because it surfaced in a state where his attorney general hails from and is the brainchild of the man Trump appointed in May 2017 to be vice-chair of his Advisory Commission on Election Integrity, Kansas Secretary of State, Kris Kobach. Vice President Mike Pence is the panel's titular chairman. Kobach built his career by targeting the nonwhite populations that Republicans want to suppress in elections and now has a White House–sanctioned podium.[142]

Paper proof of citizenship emerged a dozen years ago in Arizona. Kobach, then a lawyer and anti-immigrant activist in his late thirties, saw that adding it to the Republican catalog of voting "reforms" could help launch a political career. And it did. He helped draft a ballot measure in 2004, Arizona's Proposition 200, which included requiring citizenship proof to register for state elections.[143] Around this time, Kobach and his allies sued three states for not charging higher out-of-state tuition rates to the undocumented students at state colleges and universities (they lost in court). He later befriended Maricopa County's anti-immigrant Sheriff Joe Arpaio and helped draft a state law letting police demand proof of immigration status to anyone pulled over in a traffic stop.[144] Arizona voters passed Prop. 200 in 2004, starting a legal fight that most people thought ended in 2013 when the Supreme Court threw out most of the law.[145] But Kobach—this decade's Thor Hearne—doesn't take no for an answer.

During the race for Kansas secretary of state, his campaign website claimed that voter fraud had "burrowed into every corner of our country" and "illegal registration of alien voters has become pervasive" in his state.[146] Weeks after taking office in 2011, Kobach convinced his legislature to adopt a tougher voter ID law and to require registrants to provide paper proof of citizenship.[147] (They later gave him power to prosecute voter fraud, unlike any other secretary of state.) Kobach found like-minded Republicans in Alabama, Georgia, and Arizona. They did not need to be told the benefits of raising the bar to participate in state elections. In 2009, Georgia had passed its proof of citizenship law.[148] In 2011, Alabama passed its law. Arizona Republicans, meanwhile, did not let the Supreme Court's 2013 ruling stop them from instituting the proof in its elections.

Two years later, this cadre launched a sly maneuver. The secretaries of state in Arizona and Kansas followed a suggestion in the

majority opinion written by Justice Antonin Scalia that there might be
another way to achieve their goal. The states sued an obscure federal
agency, the US Election Assistance Commission (EAC), whose pur-
view included the federal voter registration form.[149] These Republicans
did not just want stricter voter requirements and applications for
their states. They wanted the federal agency to modify its registration
form to help them impose the requirement—and give its imprimatur
so other states might follow. It sounds like splitting hairs, but state
and federal elections are different legal silos. Kobach and his allies
were retreating to state's rights terrain over how they ran their state
elections. But they also sought a stamp of approval and help from a
federal agency that oversees federal elections.[150] In 2016, a Kobach
ally who became EAC executive director, Kansan Brian Newby, unilaterally changed the instructions for the federal form to add citizenship demands by Alabama, Georgia, and Kansas. That was met with
more lawsuits—where the Brennan Center, representing the League
of Women Voters in these states, submitted filings saying 7 percent of
voters do not readily have paper proof.[151] Their filing said Kobach's
hurdles had blocked thousands of Kansans from voting.

That 7 percent figure is worth repeating. That is what's at stake
in this arcane fight. Preempting another 7 percent of eligible voters
who the GOP believes tilt to the left comes after redistricting's built-in
advantage of 6 or more percentage points. It is on top of stricter voter
ID laws that add additional 2–3 percent of November election advantage—with a higher percentage advantage against non-white ethnici-
ties. It is apart from the millions of ex-felons whose voting rights have
not been restored. These are all ways that the GOP cumulatively targets the opposition. Many Democrats do not realize how these factors
add up. The proof of citizenship fight hasn't gone away because the
stakes are huge if the GOP can find a way to nullify signing one's name
as a legal oath to register to vote.

In September 2016, a federal court blocked Newby's action. In
early 2017, a court told the EAC to assess whether Newby had the

authority to do what he did.[152] That means this fight is not over. There's more evidence of that conclusion back in Kansas. The ACLU has sued Kobach for a new program called Birth Link, which seeks to automate the proof of citizenship process by comparing voter applications to state birth records. That discriminates against otherwise eligible voters born outside Kansas, one more example of his nativism.[153]

Like Trump, Kobach has said millions of noncitizens voted in 2016, but he can't offer any proof—as there is none.[154] But in the GOP's prejudice-filled world of voting, we have seen facts don't matter—even if research repeatedly proves it. In May 2017, the Brennan Center released a report to rebut Trump's claims of immigrants illegally voting. It looked in forty-two jurisdictions in twelve states with the country's largest noncitizen populations. Out of 23.5 million votes cast in those jurisdictions in 2016, election offices could only cite thirty instances of "suspected noncitizen voting," noting that figure was "0.0001 percent of the votes cast."[155]

"In California, Virginia, and New Hampshire—the states where Trump claimed the problem of noncitizen voting was especially acute—no [election] official we spoke with identified any incidents of noncitizen voting in 2016," the Center said. But during the 2016 campaign and afterward, Kobach stood by Trump's big lie. You can be sure the proof of citizenship charade will resurface as he cochairs the White House's "election integrity" commission. While the panel's work is likely to be ignored like past presidential panels, Kobach has continued to promote outright falsehoods as partisan gospel.

Days after Trump named Kobach to his commission, *The New York Times* reported that he "declared victory in the fraud wars" by claiming he had unearthed 125 non-citizens out of 1.8 million registered voters in Kansas.[156] That's 0.007 percent of its voters. Many of the noncitizens never voted, the *Times* said, but reported their mistake to local officials. "Most of Mr. Kobach's nine fraud convictions involve people who voted in two states," it said. "Neither a citizenship requirement nor an ID would have prevented those offenses."

But Kobach did accomplish partisan goals. When a federal court struck down some of his restrictions in 2016, it said these laws "denied more than 18,000 Kansans their constitutional right to cast ballots," according to the *Times*. "Whenever I hear Kris Kobach use the words 'voter fraud,' what that means in English for regular folks is voter suppression," Rep. Jim Ward, Kansas House Minority Leader, told the newspaper. "Most secretaries of state see their job to be a fair arbiter of elections. Kris has believed that the secretary of state is a partisan tool to affect the results of elections."

ANOTHER HIJACKED STATE: GEORGIA

IN THE 2016 CYCLE, THERE WERE other examples of Republican secretaries of state targeting the registration process to suppress votes. Georgia's Republicans showcased bad behavior in 2016—just as it did in the 2014–15 cycle. Georgia is another state whose complexion would be purple were it not for aggressive efforts by Republicans to preempt voters and stymie voting to keep its rule red. This pattern can be seen locally and at the highest reaches of state government.

One eyebrow-raising local example came in 2015, when white Republicans in rural Hancock County, who are a majority on its county board of elections, sent sheriff deputies knocking on the front doors of more than 180 black voters in the town of Sparta. They were not concerned about real crime; they were questioning voter registrations.[157] Their goal in dogging one-fifth of the town's voters was to help a white mayoral candidate, a lawsuit that followed said. The county attorney, a Republican state legislator, defended the police action by alleging sloppy voter rolls. This was intimidation by whites to keep blacks from voting.

While Sparta was a local drama, a fight with statewide consequences involving registrations broke out that same year between Georgia's Republican Secretary of State, Brian Kemp, and its House

Minority Leader, Democrat Stacey Abrams. Seen from afar, it looked like Kemp was modernizing the process by instituting online voter registration that year. But Abrams was leading an effort called the New Georgia Project that was running traditional voter drives, where canvassers went door-to-door and registrants filled out paper forms. In October 2014, it emerged that more than forty-one thousand of the eighty-seven thousand forms filed by the Project were not going to be processed by Election Day.[158]

This disclosure was not accompanied by the usual gripe from local officials about voter drives—that activists dump mountains of paper on their desks at the last minute. Instead, Kemp announced he was launching a major voter fraud investigation as one of his state's biggest drives in years was cresting. That accusation and the bureaucratic stonewalling that ensued was completely disingenuous. His investigation, completed months after Election Day, found problems with twenty-five of the eighty-seven thousand voter forms submitted—0.03 percent. But there's far more that Kemp did to block voters in the 2015–2016 cycle.

Remember the data fields that comprise what information is required to register—one's name, address, birth date, and driver's license or Social Security number? Kemp deliberately politicized a process that is similar to what is used in many states. When people do not register online, local election offices end up typing the information from paper forms into computers and the statewide voter file. Beyond illegible handwriting and typos that occur—and cause some people to not be registered—local officials also do electronic checks to verify the information. States validate a would-be voter's identity by pinging their driver's license database and the federal Social Security database using the last four digits of an applicant's Social Security number. Some also ping prison records to screen for felons. Under Kemp, any unconfirmed match rejected the registrants.

Where this becomes insidious is every one of those databases has had known accuracy problems or shortcomings that disqualify eligible voters. In 2009, the Social Security Administration (SSA)

Inspector General's office assessed how reliable its voter verification was. Compared to "other [Social Security number-based verification] programs used by the states and employers . . . (the voter registration) no-match rate was two-to-five times higher," rejecting an additional 16 percent of registrants, it found. Why? That bigger gap was because other SSA programs used the full nine-digit Social Security number, while the voter registration program only used the last four digits. Less precise matching yields more errors.[159]

In 2005, Congress's GAO issued a report finding state drivers license databases confuse names, including full names, names with or without middle initials, aliases, etc. "Even a 1 percent error rate on a match validating names, driver license numbers, etc., could generate tens of thousands of bad matches," the nonpartisan congressional analysts reported.[160]

The Atlanta-Journal Constitution noted on how this process unfolded in their state in late 2014. "If everything goes right, a match comes back and the voter's name is sent to the Secretary of State's Office. But it sometimes does not go right," they wrote.[161] They cited the problems with Social Security and drivers' license data, and noted why state prison records also were unreliable. "County officials must also ping the state Department of Corrections database, which may lag by up to several months in its information," the paper wrote. "The Social Security Administration database only comes back as a 'yes' or 'no' match, giving county officials no help in determining what further information may need to be provided by the applicant. A hyphenated last name can cause hiccups with the state's identification database, as can unintentional data entry errors by county clerks, said former North Carolina [state] election director Gary Bartlett, who submitted an affidavit on behalf of the voter groups [who sued over the botched processing of registrations]."[162]

In other words, Kemp did not just masquerade behind the badge of fighting nonexistent voter fraud to thwart a registration drive led by a powerful elected Democrat. He also was winnowing voter rolls to impact the finish line—who can vote on Election Day. And there's more. Between October 2012 and November 2014, he purged more than 370,000 inactive voters, which exceeded the number of newly registered voters.[163] But at the starting line, voter registration, he was knowingly using a shoddy verification process to disqualify or hold registrants in limbo. Using porous data and imprecise analytics produces a politically expedient result: false positives. A lawsuit over Kemp's matching that was settled in early 2017 found that of the nearly thirty-five thousand registrants whose registrations he canceled between July 2013 and July 15, 2016, 64 percent were black, 8 percent were Latino, 5 percent were Asian, and 14 percent were white.[164] Meanwhile, of those forty-one thousand registrants that Kemp kept from voting in 2014, eighteen thousand were approved *after* the election in which they registered to vote. This is how nuanced and targeted voter suppression works.

Kemp's tactics, especially using error-prone data mining, are not unique. One of its biggest proponents is Kobach, who, as Kansas secretary of state, oversees the Interstate Voter Registration Crosscheck Program. That project was created in 2005 by state election directors with the goal of identifying voters registered in more than one state and instances of illegal double voting. It does so by matching first and last names, birth dates, and state turnout data.[165] It was used by twenty-five states in 2016. You would be correct if you concluded that it surfaces hardly any illegal activity—single-digit instances from states each with tens of millions of voters. But its imprecise methodology generates hundreds of thousands of false positives.

In 2015, Crosscheck *helped* Kemp identify some 540,000 Georgia voters[166] who were in danger of being purged before the 2016 election. That's one-eighth of the Georgians who voted for president that fall. This points to another fight in the lead up to the election—mass purges by GOP secretaries of state of tens of thousands of infrequent but legally registered voters in Democratic strongholds. In early 2017, Georgia and more than a dozen red states filed a brief at the Supreme Court urging it to hear a case in its fall term over Ohio's purge of

144,000 infrequent voters in blue epicenters before the 2016 election. These red states sided with Ohio's partisan mass purge.[167] The Supreme Court will hear the case, where Ohio acted after exploiting another ambiguity in federal voting laws.

Meanwhile, the battle between Georgia Secretary of State Brian Kemp and House Minority Leader Stacey Abrams is not over. Both are running for governor in 2018 (as is Kobach in Kansas). But the tactic that Kemp and Kobach engaged in—targeting and freezing out new voters, and partisan purges of infrequent voters—is the next stage in the process where the GOP has an indisputable record of cynically exploiting a simple bookkeeping process.

12

THE FINISH LINE

THE DEEPER WE DELVE INTO DETAILS, the more we see the GOP hijack technicalities. One of the most persistent is selectively purging voters, which is when registered voters are removed from voter rolls under the guise of keeping the lists current. When these voters show up to vote in states without Election Day registration, they are told they can reregister for the next election—but they can not vote that day. Many protest and poll workers end up giving them provisional ballots. But those ballots are usually disqualified and don't count.

There are many legitimate reasons to keep rolls up-to-date by removing names, especially in our mobile society. List maintenance, as it's called, streamlines the process at the polls, saving counties and campaigns money on printing ballots and mailings, and helps with planning for turnout at precincts. But what should be routine book-keeping can also be darkly politicized.

There are other recent examples where Republicans combined their propagandistic voter fraud meme and sought to use, or did use, sloppy analytics to target legal voters for mass removals. An especially eyebrow-raising example came from Florida in 2014, when GOP Secretary of State Ken Detzner scrapped a statewide purge after county officials openly rejected his attempt to impose mistake-ridden purge lists on them.[168]

That rebellion was a remarkable development in the usually com-
pliant world of election officials. But Florida is not just any state when
it comes to purges. It got a black eye after the 2000 election for a catalog
of dysfunction. One of its worst episodes involved Florida Secretary of
State (and George W. Bush campaign cochair) Katherine Harris. She
hired a contractor, Database Technologies, to winnow the state's voter
rolls.[169] The National Voter Registration Act lays out what counties are
supposed to do, which, needless to say, Florida didn't do. The NVRA says
no registered voter is to be removed unless they have not voted in four
years—two full federal cycles—and only after postcards were mailed to
them advising them they were being placed on inactive lists and could be
purged if they do not resume voting.[170] The 1993 law also says infrequent
voting is not a sufficient reason to be removed from official lists, creating
an ambiguity that's come under GOP attack—but more on that later.

What Harris did was piggyback on another racist legacy, Florida's
lifetime voting ban for felons. While denying the vote to felons has
constitutional precedents, it has been twisted in a handful of states
to disenfranchise an outsized percent of nonwhites—especially nonviolent drug offenders in the war on drugs. In 2000, more than eight
hundred thousand Floridians, about 7.5 percent of its voting-age population, had permanently lost their voting rights this way. (The figure
in 2016 is double that: 1.6 million citizens, including 21 percent of
voting age blacks.[171]) Harris hired Database Technologies to create a
list of "possible" and "probable felons" who were on Florida's rolls.
It presented her office with 82,389 names, which was 1 percent of its
electorate. In turn, she instructed county election officials to remove
the voters who Database Technologies identified.

"The tallies were wildly inaccurate," wrote Michael Waldman in
his book, *The Fight to Vote*. "The search used primitive methods, such
as identifying voters who share a common name and birth date with
someone who had a criminal record." Thousands of legitimate voters
were wrongly purged in the race where the Supreme Court stopped
a recount and George W. Bush "won" by 537 votes.[172] In his book,

Give Us The Ballot, Ari Berman said that "no one could ever determine precisely how many voters who were incorrectly labeled felons were turned away from the polls." He notes a legal settlement between the NAACP and Florida re-ran Harris's purge list with "stricter criteria" and found twelve thousand errors.[173] More than poorly designed ballots—where hundreds of Palm Beach County Democrats mistakenly voted for Pat Buchanan—the purge was a bigger factor in tilting the odds to Bush via a hidden administrative process.

Fast forward to 2012 when Detzner revived Harris's script with a twist. He swapped her fear of felons with his fear of noncitizens. Two years before, Detzner, whom Republican Gov. Rick Scott appointed, claimed that there were 180,000 possible noncitizen voters based on state driver's license records. After pushback by voting rights advocates that number shrank to 2,600, and then to 200, and finally 85 people were removed from Florida's voter rolls. In 2014, Detzner tried again. This time, he wanted to use a federal Department of Homeland Security database to identify noncitizens, even though the agency said it was incomplete. While Detzner and DHS argued in court, his county election supervisors refused to accept purge lists from Florida's state election director. Their routine list maintenance process worked, they said. They didn't need a solution for a nonexistent problem.[174]

You would think in the relatively small world of election administration that such brazen moves would be known and widely rejected. But across the country, local election officials rarely are that bold—or some agree with the GOP's goals. In mid-2016, Kim Strach, the North Carolina Board of Elections executive director, also appointed by Republicans, used a PowerPoint demonstration to augment her testimony before her GOP-run legislature. It said 35,750 voters were "registered in North Carolina and another state and voted in both [states for the] 2012 general election," Greg Palast noted in August 2016's *Rolling Stone*.[175]

Where did her number originate? In part, the Interstate Crosscheck program run by Kobach. Under media scrutiny, Strach backtracked. "We were not suggesting that 35,750 voters had committed any type of fraud," she told Palast. "There were 35,750 people who voted in North Carolina whose first and last names and dates of birth matched persons who voted in the same election in another state." Strach was using porous data and knew it. "Despite hiring an ex-FBI agent to lead the hunt, the state has charged exactly zero double voters from the Crosscheck list," the *Rolling Stone* article said.

Palast then quoted Mark Swedlund, a "database expert whose clients include eBay and American Express," who was stunned after looking at Crosscheck's Georgia and Virginia lists. "God forbid your name is Garcia, of which there are 858,000 in the US, and your first name is Joseph or Jose. You're probably suspected of voting in 27 states," he said. Their point is partisan purges based on flimsy data are another large-scale means to take out eligible Democrats when the number of purged voters can exceed margins of victory.

What's emerged since Palast's report is that North Carolina, through Crosscheck, had identified 455,891 suspicious voters as of February 2016. In Ohio, it identified 386,092 suspicious registrations. In Michigan, it was 406,268. In Arizona, it was 240,277. In the twenty-five participating states analyzed in 2016, more than 5.9 million registrants were flagged as suspicious by this Republican-led fishing expedition that pretends to protect the integrity of the vote as a supposedly effective administrative bookkeeping tool. These figures are from a March 2017 brief filed at the Supreme Court by Republican former Justice Department officials, including those who led the Bush administration's voter fraud witch hunts. They urged the Court to hear a case over Ohio Republicans' mass purge of hundreds of thousands of infrequent voters between 2012 and 2016.[176]

In June 2017, the Court took the case, which will be heard in their fall 2017 term. In *A. Phillip Randolph Institute v. Husted*, Ohio's Republican Secretary of State Jon Husted is appealing a September 2016 federal appeals court ruling that found the purges he ordered violated the NVRA. Husted created a "so-called 'Supplemental Process,'" the ruling said, to identify all voters who had not voted in two years and put them on a track for removal.[177] The Appeals Court said Ohio should not have purged infrequent voters—as many people only turn out in presidential elections every four years. A dissenting opinion said the NVRA was "ambiguous," because, on one hand it laid out a process to remove voters who did not show up for four years—two federal cycles, but on the other hand it also said voters could not be removed "by reason of the person's failure to vote."

This ambiguity was seized and exploited by Husted—just as Republicans in other states seized upon the lack of a definitive federal citizenship database to demand paper proof of citizenship. Under Husted, Ohio has a notorious record for purging voters. As Ari Berman noted in *The Nation* after the Supreme Court said it would hear the NVRA case, "From 2011 to 2016, Ohio purged 2 million voters from the rolls—1.2 million for infrequent voting—more than any other state."[178] The purges have unabashedly favored Republicans. In June 2016, Reuters reported that twice as many voters were purged in "Democratic-leaning neighborhoods" compared to "Republican-leaning" neighborhoods in the counties where Ohio's three biggest cities are located—Cleveland, Cincinnati, and Columbus.[179]

"The disparity is especially stark in Hamilton County, where affluent Republican suburbs ring Cincinnati, which has one of the highest child-poverty rates in the country," Reuters reported. "In the heavily African-American neighborhoods near downtown, more than 10 percent of registered voters have been removed due to inactivity since 2012. In suburban Indian Hill, only 4 percent have been purged due to inactivity."

This disparity is another facet of what twenty-first-century voter suppression looks like. Democrats are targeted and peeled away, a few percentage points at a time. After the Sixth Circuit Court of Appeals ruled against Husted in September 2016, 7,500 of the purged Ohio voters were restored. (That's because the NVRA prohibits removals within ninety days of a federal election.[180]) But that victory only restored a fraction of the otherwise eligible voters who were removed.

It underscores how the GOP benefits by throwing the most destructive first punches in a voting rights war of attrition.

When thinking about Ohio's purges, Crosscheck's use in North Carolina, Georgia's use of imprecise voter verification databases, or Florida's bid to seize any government file to find noncitizens, one must not only ask why are Republicans doing everything within reach to obstruct voting. One also must ask why are voter file procedures and systems so prone to partisan abuses? Why are they so outdated and unsophisticated compared to private-sector data mining, which tracks people's identity, address, and contact information, and lets no online search go unrewarded without deluging the searcher with banner ads?

Part of the answer is politicians don't want to change a system that they mastered—and that serves them. That is also true with the federal campaign finance system. As a result, elections often are kept as a backwater in state and federal budgets. They are underfunded and have aging voting machines that are hardly ever replaced. That takes on added significance when we look at the computer systems used—some of which were targeted by Russians in the run-up to 2016's Election Day.

But mostly, Republicans don't want high turnout elections—and that starts with registration. In 2010, I briefly worked with the Pew Center on the States as part of its Voter Registration Modernization Design Working Group. It was clear that states could use better data to verify registrations—such as changes of address from credit rating agencies and the post office.[181] It was also clear states could find and register all eligible voters if there was the political will—which Oregon later did. Pew devised a plan for a far better data-mining operation than Crosscheck that top state election officials could convince legislatures to use. It was a way to make rolls more accurate, efficiently managed, and cost-effective. But it wouldn't automatically register voters, even though it identified all of the eligible but unregistered voters in participating states.

Red state election directors said they could only take eligible voters up to the finish line, but those people would have to cross it on their own. They talked about citizens taking the final affirmative step. That's as far as sympathetic Republicans went. Under Pew's blueprint, the participating states would identify all their eligible voters and contact them to urge them to register. It also used better data to maintain voter rolls under the NVRA's timetable. The system it created, called ERIC—Electronic Registration Information System—was used by twenty states in 2016.[182] Some of these states are also in Crosscheck's network, but do not use Crosscheck's data due to its shortcomings. ERIC was a reason why 200 million people were registered to vote in 2016. (Notably, no ERIC states are represented on Trump's election integrity commission led by Kobach.) But registration alone is not the key to winning. REDMAP showed it's not just about candidates and registrations, but getting a reliable base to the polls in sufficient numbers. Clinton's presidential campaign showed you could not alienate a sizable slice of your party's base and get all of them to turn out.

Predictably, as the 2016 election traversed from summer into fall and Clinton led in the polls, Trump began making repeated claims that the election would be stolen by voter fraud. "More than 1.8 million deceased individuals, right now, are listed as voters," he said, citing Pew's work.[183] Of course, that Pew study never made claims about the dead voting; it was intended to show dead weight that needed to be removed by modernizing how voter rolls are maintained—part of making a case for ERIC. But, as the right-wing blogosphere is wont to do, that statistic was distorted and exaggerated. By January 2017, Trump's Press Secretary Sean Spicer said, "There's one report that came out of Pew in 2008 that showed 14 percent of people who voted were noncitizens." That Pew issue brief, also created to promote the need for ERIC, did not mention noncitizens either.[184]

But facts don't matter when it comes to the voter fraud meme: double voters, dead voters, noncitizen voters, whatever. As a former Florida Republican Party chairman, Jim Greer, told the *Palm Beach Post* in 2012, voter ID laws and cutbacks in early voting were "done for one reason and one reason only," to suppress the Democrats. Greer remarked Florida's Republican political consultants "never came in to see me and tell me we had a fraud issue. It's all a marketing ploy."[185]

America is nothing if not a marketing society. It's unclear how much Trump's revival of the voter fraud meme motivated his voters, apart from inflaming anti-Clinton sentiments among swing voters or preaching to the GOP's converted. A poll in mid-September 2016 from the *Washington Post*–ABC News found that nearly half of registered voters across the country believed voter fraud occurs "somewhat" or "very" often. As *The New York Times* editorialized about that finding, "Another 26 percent of American voters said that fraud 'rarely' occurs, but even that characterization is off the mark. Just 1 percent of respondents gave the answer that comes closest to reality: Never.'"[186]

By October, Trump wasn't just tweeting, "Stop Crooked Hillary From Rigging This Election!" He was trying to recruit "Trump Election Observers" to police the polls. As in past presidential years, Trump was sending out a call for GOP loyalists to go to precincts in blue strongholds and challenge the credentials of anyone who didn't appear to them to be a legitimate voter. There's a long history of Jim Crow-era incidents of this ilk. But beyond the GOP putting up billboards in recent cycles in minority neighborhoods in battleground states[187] threatening arrest should someone not present the proper voter ID—another lie—this is more bark than bite. Still, there were a few overt voter vigilantes in 2016.

VOTING VIGILANTES

MOST POLICE-THE-POLLS THREATS REMAIN JUST THAT—THREATS to discourage voting. But North Carolina saw a notable vigilante effort as the 2016 Election Day approached. A longtime right-wing activist, Jay DeLancy, who runs a group called Voter Integrity Project of North Carolina, targeted thousands of voters to be purged from three counties with large black populations. What he did is called caging—a tactic the Republican National Committee was caught doing in the 1990s, and signed a federal consent decree agreeing to stop. In 2013, DeLancy told a local weekly newspaper, "I can't be a Republican and do what I'm doing." But, of course, he is a Republican—and an activist in a state where party and race overlap.[188] DeLancy said TrueTheVote, a Tea Party-based group that started in Houston, Texas, and sees itself as a polling place posse, had inspired him. TrueTheVote subsequently failed to go national in 2012.

Delancy's group specialized in a tactic that's an electoral mugging. They sent postcards to addresses of registered voters in three key counties—people who had not voted recently. The postcards said, "do not forward" and thousands were therefore returned. They took those cards to county election offices as "evidence" to challenge those voters' registrations. The NAACP heard about this and sued. One week before the 2016 election, a federal judge ordered the counties to restore 6,700 voters.[189]

US District Judge Loretta Biggs ordered the State Board of Elections to restore voters who had been purged within ninety days of the fall election.[190] Needless to say, county election boards knew the NVRA's procedures—it's been law since 1993. They should have ignored DeLancy's vigilantism. However, the voter suppressor, in remarks that echoed Kobach's ongoing proof-of-citizenship gambit, hewed to a state's rights line. "The state did nothing wrong with following the law. We did nothing wrong in following the law," DeLancy told the Associated Press. The wire service wrote, "he hopes the federal voting rules that Biggs cited in her ruling are ultimately challenged." DeLancy had plenty of company among North Carolina's voter suppressors. At the GOP-run State Board of Elections, staff attorney Josh Lawson said it would comply with the court order but might "appeal facets of the ruling, potentially after the election."

Sloppy partisan purges, using bad voter data in accusatory ways, taking preemptive steps to deprive others of voting rights—these tactics are taken for granted by fervent Republicans in North Carolina and elsewhere. They persist despite forceful court rulings in the past two years, starting with rejecting race-based gerrymanders in North Carolina, Texas, Alabama, and Virginia. Federal Courts have overturned other anti-voter laws in states like Wisconsin, Pennsylvania, and Kansas. But North Carolina stood apart in 2016—even surpassing Texas, where courts have struck down laws as racially discriminatory and Republicans keep trying to reinstate them.[191]

In July 2016, a federal appeals court threw out five North Carolina anti-voter laws that its opinion said "target African-Americans with almost surgical precision." These included a more restrictive voter ID requirement, reduced early-voting options, and fewer registration opportunities, from eliminating same-day registration to blocking teenagers from registering before they turn eighteen. All were adopted after the Supreme Court gutted the Voting Rights Act in 2013.[192] Less than a year later in spring 2017, the Supreme Court refused to hear the state's appeal—saying it would reserve the right to return to those issues another time, but not in a state with such messy politics. Later that term, the Court ruled in two cases that North Carolina's redistricting was illegally racist—for two House seats and twenty-eight state legislative seats.[193]

What unfolded in North Carolina as the 2016 election crested was as brazen as any of the Republican actions to seize or hold power this decade. It showed that as the pendulum swung back toward voting rights, the GOP had no reluctance to impede nonwhites and Democrats from voting, to disqualify their votes, and to overturn results. North Carolina's story is even more remarkable because before REDMAP targeted it in 2010, it had the most progressive and inclusive voting laws in the South. It was politically purple, but the Republicans viciously rolled back the clock to turn its complexion red.

All of that was apart from what the Russians may also have been doing in North Carolina by targeting its voting systems. As of late spring 2017, there were questions if hacking could have scrambled voter registration data and e-poll books in Durham County, which may have led to computer breakdowns, delays for voters, and the necessity for poll workers to turn to paper ballots.[194] When asked what caused that those snafus, Durham County BOE staff quickly rejected hacking and blamed "user error."[195] That's voters and poll workers—anyone but those actually responsible for managing the voting systems.

13

THE PLAYBOOK: DO EVERYTHING

As THE ELECTION CAME TO A close, other factors outside of the fine print of voting undoubtedly helped Trump and the GOP. These included former FBI Director James Comey announcing in late October that the bureau was reopening its investigation into Clinton's handling of her classified email as US secretary of state, her campaign's decision not to step up Clinton's visits in Michigan and Wisconsin, the still-simmering rifts between her supporters and the Sanders camp, and the continuing leaks of Clinton campaign emails by Wikileaks—which federal intelligence agencies blamed on Russian hacking. Meanwhile, beyond Trump's taunts to "Lock her up" and rants that Democrats always steal millions of votes,[196] the GOP in a handful of states kept returning to the voter fraud meme to tilt the results their way.

States we haven't discussed much, like Arizona, enacted new barriers to complicate the process. In mid-2016, Arizona made it a felony to collect and turn in another person's absentee ballot. That targeted seniors, especially in Latino communities. Indiana deputized party officials to patrol polling places and demand voters to show their IDs, another intimidation tactic. In Marion County, where Indianapolis is its largest city and many blacks live, GOP election officials only opened one early voting site, compared to more than twenty in adjacent white suburban counties.[197] In all, fourteen states had new restrictions on the process as Election Day approached.[198] In North Carolina, where a federal court in July 2016 threw out anti-voter laws passed after the Supreme Court gutted the Voting Rights Act, the state's GOP drew on its playbook and showed no tactic was too shameless when power was at stake.

As the November vote approached, North Carolina's Republican-dominated government and election bureaucracy were already ignoring the federal court ruling that its post-VRA laws were illegally racist. It revived Jim Crow era tactics simply making it harder to vote. Black turnout was down 16 percent during the first week of early voting because "in heavily black counties, there were 158 fewer early polling places," *The Nation's* Joan Walsh reported.[199] On Monday before Election Day, the state party issued a release bragging about this result. "African-American early voting is down 8.5 percent from this time in 2012. Caucasian voters early voting is up 22.5 percent from this time in 2012." The GOP spun this as a sign that Obama's coalition was "crumbing."[200]

It's worth revisiting fine print in that July 2016 court ruling because it is microcosm of the motives and strategies embodied in the GOP's war on voters during this decade. Despite its extreme redistricting in 2011, US Court of Appeals Judge Diana Gribbon Motz wrote that North Carolina was trending purple until the Supreme Court gutted the VRA in 2013. "African American registration and turnout rates had finally reached near-parity with white registration and turnout rates. African Americans were poised to act as a major electoral force," she wrote for the three-judge appeals panel.[201]

Nonetheless, the state's Legislature and governor moved "within days" to pass laws that "target African-Americans with almost surgical precision . . . and, in fact, impose cures for [alleged voter fraud] problems that did not exist," the ruling said, recounting the history. It then cited another federal ruling about similar illegal tactics in Texas—that state's post-VRA voter ID law—where "the state took away [minority voters'] opportunity because [they] were about to exercise it."[202] That's as clear an affirmation of institutional racism in elections as any federal court is apt to make.

Judge Motz didn't stop there. She named the Republicans' motives: To roll back the clock to segregationist days. North Carolina's GOP had been waiting years to do this. Between 1980 and 2013, the DOJ had rejected "Fifty proposed election law changes," the ruling noted, while voting rights groups had won fifty-five cases under the Voting Rights Act. "The legislation came into being within days of North Carolina's release from the pre-clearance requirements of the Voting Rights Act. That long-ago history bears more heavily here than it might otherwise," she wrote for the majority.[203]

Motz's opinion would not call the GOP outright racists: "Our conclusion does not mean, and we do not suggest, that any member of the General Assembly harbored racial hatred or animosity toward any minority group." But it did say that the GOP laws targeted "voters who, based on race, were unlikely to vote for the majority party." That contradiction is imbued in southern politics—taking a genteel stance that a person is not racist even if their actions have racist consequences. But the ruling's footnotes were not blind to that reality and showed some Republicans were unabashedly power hungry, racist, or both.

Judge Motz's appeals court ruling came in response to a lower federal district court ruling that upheld the anti-voter laws passed immediately after the Supreme Court gutted the VRA. The appellate court chastised the district court for acting as if it was still 1955 and segregation reigned.

"The district court took no issue with one of the Legislature's stated purposes . . . to 'move the law back to the way it was,'" Motz wrote. The accompanying footnote was stunning.[204] It quoted a "Republican precinct chairman who testified before the House Rules Committee that the photo ID requirement would 'disenfranchise some special voting blocks [sic]' and that 'that in itself is the reason to vote for the photo ID, period, end of discussion.'" That GOP precinct chairman was Don

Yelton, an AM talk radio host who called himself the Rush Limbaugh of western North Carolina. He told Comedy Central's *The Daily Show* in late 2013, "If [the law] hurts the whites so be it. If it hurts a bunch of lazy blacks that want government to give them everything, so be it."[205]

"The sheer outrageousness of these public statements by a party leader does provide some evidence of the racial and partisan political environment in which the General Assembly enacted the law," that footnote ended, returning to the cautious wording of federal court decisions.[206] As expected, North Carolina's GOP vehemently denounced the court and ruling, saying Democrats had appointed Motz and her colleagues.

But they were not the only red state getting slapped for anti-voter actions in 2016. The same day of the North Carolina ruling, federal District Court Judge James Peterson struck down some Wisconsin laws, writing "a preoccupation with mostly phantom election fraud leads to real incidents of disenfranchisement."[207] A week earlier, Texas reached a settlement with the DOJ and civil rights groups to loosen its new voter ID rules after being sued for racial discrimination.[208] For a moment, it seemed like the pendulum in this decade's voting rights war was swinging back in the direction of civil rights.

These rulings should have been the end of the story, but they were not. As Election Day neared, North Carolina was like many states. Despite a close governor's race, Clinton and its Democratic US Senate candidate, Deborah Ross, a former state ACLU director and state representative, were ahead in polls. Reporters like *The Nation's* Walsh were upbeat about "a new South led by North Carolina." She mentioned repeated visits by President Obama and the First Lady, by Vice President Joe Biden, and by Bill Clinton to fight "powerful headwinds, given the state's herculean efforts at voter suppression."[209]

We know what happened. On November 8, Clinton lost the state by nearly 4 points. Ross, like the five other Senate candidates who were key to regaining a majority in that body, also lost. In the governor's race, the incumbent Republican, Pat McCrory, was trailing the

Democratic state Attorney General Roy Cooper. As results trickled in—each county had to count its regular ballots, provisional ballots, absentee, and overseas votes—McCrory's campaign consultants began accusing Democrats of voter fraud. Hundreds were named as illegal voters in vote-contesting filings and were smeared in the press. The state party filed an emergency motion with the US Supreme Court, under a complex theory it might get a ruling throwing the selection of the next governor to the GOP-led legislature.[210]

These moves showed that just when you thought the election might be over, it's not. The same was also true for Democrats across the nation who did not understand why Clinton lost—especially after polls showed her leading despite Comey's resurrection of the FBI's investigation. In Michigan, more than seventy-five thousand ballots were initially reported on the state's website as missing presidential votes. That state had the nation's tightest finish, with eleven thousand votes separating Clinton and Trump. In Wisconsin, where a tough voter ID law was in effect for April's primaries but thrown out by a federal judge in July, Trump won by nearly twenty-three thousand votes. Milwaukee County, with its largest population of blacks and tens of thousands of students, cast sixty thousand fewer votes than in 2012. (Only two years before, another court noted that an estimated three hundred thousand Wisconsin residents, mostly poor and students, lacked required IDs to get a ballot.) And in Pennsylvania, voting machines in dozens of counties that went for Trump were entirely paperless, which meant that there was no way to audit or verify the reported result.[211]

As the campaign peaked, Clinton was crestfallen by Comey's investigation, preoccupied with Russian interference, and believed that she was ahead in key Midwestern states—Michigan and Wisconsin. Her campaign sent Clinton and its resources elsewhere. These observations and miscalculations are detailed in the 2017 book *Shattered: Inside Hillary Clinton's Doomed Campaign* by Jonathan Allen and Amie Parnes.[212]

What's not in that book and most post-2016 accounts is how Democrats, including many Berniecrats, voted for Clinton—even if it was more out of opposition to Trump than affirmation of her. But she was an insider in a season favoring outsiders. The Democratic establishment anointed Clinton expecting she would be facing ex-Florida Gov. Jeb Bush. Nonetheless, many coastal Democrats rallied and believed she was more progressive than her husband. Wall Street, Silicon Valley, and even northeastern Virginia, where Pentagon contractors and federal employees live, saw her as a technocrat who understood them. But across interior America, Clinton was unconvincing for many reasons. Those ranged from her cautiousness on the stump to decades of being pilloried as an elitist, liberal feminist by right-wing media in those regions. Too many women, let alone men threatened by strong women, rejected her.

All these factors, which politically attentive Americans are aware of, played into Trump's favor. But what is overlooked in those cultural and political analyses is how the stubborn Republican game plan of doing everything to rig the rules and tilt the field comes into play when contests are tight and the turnout is less than a landslide. The 2016 election didn't see the turnout waves and popular vote margins of victory that Obama inspired in 2008 (9.5 million votes) and 2012 (5 million votes). While her 2.9 million popular vote victory was bigger numerically and percentage-wise than John Kennedy's in 1960 and Richard Nixon's in 1968, it wasn't sufficient to translate into an Electoral College victory in 2016.

Republicans turn to a do-everything strategy because our elections are so decentralized. There are ten thousand jurisdictions overseeing one hundred thousand Election Day precincts nationwide—to say nothing of states that vote early and vote by mail. It is virtually impossible to predict the final swing precincts, in the swing counties, in the swing states. No pundit, pollster, or data analytic expert accurately foresaw where she would fall short by tens of thousands of votes compared to Obama in 2012.

That's why Republicans deploy such a vast playbook of starting line advantages, such as extreme redistricting giving them upwards of a 6–8 point lead, and other barriers such as strict voter ID laws that also shave another 2–3 percent off of Democratic voting blocs in November (and even more in the primaries). Nobody precisely knows where the fault lines will appear in a country with 137 million presidential voters, especially in a year like 2016 with no final battleground state—unlike Ohio in 2004 and Florida in 2000.

While Democrats were mortified with the outcome—Trump's victory and the Democrats' loss of the Senate—the travesties didn't end on Election Night. They continued when Americans wanted to know what happened, including who voted for Trump and why. They found elections are filled with additional opacities, namely, a non-transparent vote verification process, and partisan and institutional reluctance to recount close elections.

That absence, after a race that never seemed to end, was another antidemocratic feature of our system of voting. When citizens are left grasping for facts and officials don't or won't provide them, then the most cynical, biased, and conspiratorial forces win. Voters deserved to know who voted for Trump and trust that counts were accurate—or realize why voting machinery is unreliable. The Green Party's recounts sought those answers, and they were blocked on almost every front.

SECTION III
THE RECOUNTS

14

WHAT HAPPENED?

NO DEMOCRAT OR PROGRESSIVE NEEDS TO be reminded how they felt on 2016's Election Night. During the day, precinct exit polls by a national media consortium of the print and broadcast outlets reported a tight race but likely a Clinton victory. But as results trickled in and states assumed to be reliably blue lined up behind Trump, and the GOP took control of Congress, disbelief and shock set in. At about 11:15 PM Eastern, the AP called North Carolina for Trump. A half hour later Fox News called Wisconsin for Trump. Clinton was ahead in Pennsylvania, but her strongholds had all reported and Trump was gaining. At midnight, David Simas, Obama's White House political director, called Clinton Campaign Manager Robby Mook and urged them to not "drag this out."[213]

Clinton wouldn't concede until the next morning. Immediately across America, voters, campaign volunteers, and others who did not imagine a Trump victory and GOP sweep, did not accept this result. The public, especially Democrats, wanted to know what happened, what went wrong and hoped there might be some way to prevent Trump and GOP from taking power in January 2017. An angst-filled campaign ended with even more angst.

Just when explanations and understanding were needed, mainstream media failed to deliver. The biggest outlets, which for months hawked their latest polls as gospel, did not discuss what they had missed or misreported. Nor did they consider pausing to verify the results in swing states, where, only days before, polls had projected Clinton as winning. Instead, the outlets did what they always do in the aftermath of close and controversial elections. They seized upon an easy narrative to explain away the results, while ignoring a genuine desire for actual proof. The most seized-upon narrative was low-income, working-class whites came out for Trump in a spasm to preserve their place in an increasingly diverse nation. (By mid-2017, academics found Trump's base was white but was not low-income; most lacked college degrees but two-thirds made more than $50,000 (just below America's median household income), with a third making more than $100,000.)[214]

What ensued after November 8 was schizophrenic. Beyond the GOP hyping Trump's win as a mandate and Trump blaring he would have won the popular vote if millions of immigrants had not voted illegally—a lie—state election directors saw November 8 as a wide success. Compared to 2012, the top officials said there were fewer delays and polling place problems. Across the country, voting in communities of color and white areas was more similar than not, they added, applauding themselves.[215] These same officials spent the fall downplaying reports that Russians had breached their computerized voting systems. By spring 2017, it emerged that thirty-nine states were targeted and one had been penetrated—more than anyone reported during the election. But Election Day did not produce obvious telltale signs of interference, such as outsized requests for provisional ballots by voters not on precinct lists.[216] The officials overseeing elections wanted to slam the door on 2016, sweeping under the rug the less visible, anti-democratic, poorly performing, or possibly malicious features of the election. They turned to certifying the results and taking vacations.

That landscape left a handful of voting rights activists, constitutional lawyers, computer science experts, and journalists looking for answers and explanations—or offering their own. Chris Thomas, who retired in early 2017 after thirty-six years as Michigan's election director, called these people "wonks," "crusaders," and "professional irritants" in an exit interview with a trade publication, reflecting how many in his profession see these advocates.[217]

Nonetheless, one of the first analyses to emerge came from a cadre of election integrity activists who, since 2004's presidential election, have been tracking discrepancies between media exit polls and the Election Night results. (These counts are not the official totals that come days or weeks later, but unofficial ones used by the media to project winners and by the candidates to declare victory or concede.) These activists emphasized that international election observers use exit polls as a big clue for detecting fraudulent results. They were astonished. As Election Defense Alliance cofounder Jonathan Simon wrote, "By early morning [November 9] I had begun circulating tables documenting the most egregious 'red shift' exit poll to vote count disparities ever recorded in the computerized voting era. Even for those accustomed to the mysterious and pervasive rightward shifts between exit poll and vote count results, the results were eye-popping."[218]

By "red shift," Simons meant exit polls that predicted Democratic victories in contrast to results adding up to a Republican sweep. He wrote, "Ohio had shifted from an exit poll dead heat to an 8.1 percent Trump win; North Carolina from a 2.1 percent Clinton win to a 3.6 percent Trump win; Pennsylvania from 4.4 percent Clinton to 0.7 percent Trump; Wisconsin from 3.9 percent Clinton to 0.7 percent Trump; Florida from 1.3 percent Clinton to 1.2 percent Trump; and Michigan from a dead heat to 0.3 percent Trump . . . If the exit polls rather than the vote counts were accurately capturing voter intent, the Electoral College majority would have gone to Clinton and it would not have been close."[219]

Simons and his colleagues were grabbing at the only available information to question whether the counts had been hijacked. Needless to say, they believed that it had. Election officials ignored them, as did the media consortium and its pollsters. As has been the case for years, the consortium refused to release any raw precinct-level data. (During the day, they revise projections to reflect a better picture of electorate.) As number crunchers on list-serves screamed this was proof of yet another stolen election, exit pollsters countered these activists were gadflies reading too much into imperfect exit polls. (One of their team who conducted exit polls in Berkeley, California, the publisher of Ballot Access News, Richard Winger, told me that no voter he interviewed said that they had voted for Trump—but there were several who did in the official count at his precinct.) The exit poll discrepancy stalemate left a trail of dots that could not be connected without more proof, which was not forthcoming.

Another early line of inquiry came from computer scientists and voting rights lawyers who were not convinced that foreign or domestic hackers—Russians or Republicans—had not targeted and planted malware that fractionally readjusted the electronically tabulated counts. Barbara Simons, a retired IBM programmer, past president of the Association for Computing Machinery, advisor to the US Election Assistance Commission since 2008, and board chair of the advocacy group Verified Voting, suspected there was more going on than what the White House and federal intelligence agencies said. James Clapper, then National Director of Intelligence, said the spy agencies had concluded that the Russian government was behind the hacks and thefts of emails from the Democratic National Committee and Clinton campaign that were posted on Wikileaks. While that theft and publication served its purpose as anti-Clinton propaganda, FBI Director Comey and President Obama said the voting machinery was separate, secure, and that the vote count could be trusted. Simons knew the machinery was not secure. For more than a decade, her colleagues had routinely used voting machines in university classrooms to demonstrate hacking. Some reproduced those same experiments in congressional hearings as far back as 2006, where she was among those testifying to the House Committee on Administration.[220]

Barbara Simons talked to associates in North Carolina. In blue epicenters like Raleigh-Durham, there had been problems with electronic poll books producing precinct voter lists. She knew that the private contractor that had maintained that database and other state voter registration databases—Florida-based VR Systems—had been hacked by Russians.[221] Simons wondered if Russian hackers had scrambled North Carolina's poll books. As Steve Friess wrote in a lengthy piece in February 2017 for the *New Republic*, five days after November 8, Simons, Amy Rao—a Silicon Valley CEO and Democratic fund-raiser, and David Jefferson—a computer scientist at Lawrence Livermore National Laboratory—got John Podesta on a conference call to urge he "call for an official review of the election results."[222]

The scientists made the case that has been the baseline for more than a decade in activist circles seeking transparent and verifiable elections. The voting machines and tabulators installed after Florida's 2000 disaster with computer punch cards were aging, prone to inaccuracies, easily breached by hackers, maintained by private companies with partisan leanings, and, in a quarter of the country where voting systems were paperless—like most of Pennsylvania—impossible to recount. Podesta asked if they had proof the vote had been stolen. They replied no, but said a targeted audit of key counties and states would affirm who had won. Podesta demurred.[223]

Meanwhile, another line of inquiry was developing. John Bonifaz, a voting rights attorney who won a MacArthur "genius" award in the 1990s, also saw anomalies. Bonifaz was not another attorney frustrated with the prospect of a Trump presidency. He was the Green Party's lead attorney in their 2004 presidential recount in Ohio. (He also represented the Libertarian party.) When he realized that the Greens' 2016 presidential candidate, Jill Stein, could file for recounts if she and her party acted quickly, Bonifaz took on convincing her and trying to raise the legal fees. I've known John for two decades and wasn't surprised when he called a week after Election Day and asked whether I could write an article that suggested a recount could address serious questions.

"A lot is happening. We're looking at anomalies beyond the exit poll questions. We're looking at potential recounts in several states—not audits, but recounts," he said. "Jill Stein, on Sunday, said she's prepared to take this on. Only candidates can ask for recounts. She's willing to do it."

Bonifaz explained the filing deadlines and trail they hoped to follow. In Wisconsin, he said paperless machines had markedly different victory margins than scanned paper ballots. In Michigan, the secretary of state's office reported eighty-seven thousand paper ballots lacked presidential votes—almost double the number from 2012. (That would soon be adjusted to 75,335 undervotes.) In Pennsylvania, sixteen counties were using the same vote-count tabulators that computer scientists had shown a decade before were hackable. Bonifaz cited VR Systems' work in North Carolina and said there were questions about whether volumes of absentee ballots could be fabricated in Michigan, Wisconsin, and Pennsylvania. He wondered if the VR Systems hack could provide a pathway where election workers would unwittingly transport malware from voter registration databases to separate vote-counting computers. "That's the theory. It's strong enough for us to use as a basis for a recount," he said.

On November 18, AlterNet published my story suggesting that lingering questions were raising the prospect of filing for recounts in several states.[224] While Bonifaz tried to raise money for the filings, which were estimated to cost several million dollars, I reached out to state officials and others I knew from my work with Pew to see what they were hearing and knew. They frowned on Bonifaz's theories as dots that would not connect, even as they said they also were trying to figure out what had happened. "People are flailing and looking for something," a former official who ran elections in blue and red states said. He was skeptical that recounts would change anything, but suggested the Greens look at the machines' "logic and accuracy" tests. (Activists counter that's insufficient, as it doesn't reflect what happened on Election Day.)

"If they don't have them, that gives you something to poke at then," he said, before making what turned out to be the most prescient point. "What judges are looking for when you file suits is real evidence that results should be overturned. It has to be so screwed up that a judge will overturn it. That's not the same as a recount . . . recounts don't prove much."

Later that week, in the small world of election activists, it was inevitable that Bonifaz and Simons would join forces to again try to persuade Podesta to help—privately if not publicly. The Clinton campaign, like John Kerry in Ohio in 2004, met their voters' desire for answers with silence, not even suggesting they were evaluating the outcome. Alex Halderman, the director of the Center for Computer Security and Society at the University of Michigan, had listened to the first conference call with Podesta while aboard a flight. Afterward, he recruited thirty nationally known computer security experts and statisticians to join him to discuss possibly auditing the results. Some wanted to hand count seven hundred thousand ballots in twenty-nine states, saying such selective audits would provide certainty about the election. Others said auditing ten states could suffice. As the *New Republic* noted, the prospect of audits was more of an academic opportunity to examine the machinery than a legal procedure that could overturn results. Nonetheless, Halderman and the experts added credibility. A second conference call was held with Podesta, longtime Clinton adviser Jake Sullivan, DNC general counsel Marc Elias, and others.[225] By this point, Bonifaz was hoping the Clinton campaign—which had taken no public position—would quietly point major donors his way.

However, that didn't happen either. Instead, news of the conference call slipped out and was reported by *New York* magazine, which named Bonifaz and Halderman as coleaders of a likely recount effort. It wrote they "found persuasive evidence that results in Wisconsin, Michigan, and Pennsylvania may have been manipulated or hacked."[226] Needless to say, that breathy assertion was quickly seized upon by many—from Democrats in Congress to journalists to voters everywhere—as an offer of hope that somehow the election results could be challenged or even reversed. Bonifaz asked me to hold off on writing more about formally filing in those states, as he was trying to raise millions for filing and legal fees.

As the Thanksgiving holiday neared, he wasn't succeeding. Stein and the Greens decided to try to crowdfund the effort by turning to their grassroots base and frustrated voters. To everybody's surprise, starting midday Wednesday and continuing over the weekend, the Greens raised $7.3 million in donations from 161,000 online donors, and began recruiting what became ten thousand volunteers.[227] That unprecedented response for an unprecedented multistate presidential recount was treated with scorn and suspicion by mainstream media and the Republicans' top propaganda outlets, Fox News and Breitbart.com.

Even though it was starting late—two weeks after Election Day— the recounts held a faint prospect of getting some answers. Namely, were the votes cast accurately and legitimately counted? That would begin to reveal which communities had surprisingly supported Trump and the GOP, abandoned the Democrats, or had not voted at all. What ensued frustrated all those expectations. As Stein wrote in an email blast on the eve of Trump's inauguration, "We had little idea how hard the political establishment would fight against transparent, accountable elections."[228]

15

THE FINAL
SWING STATES

THE BIGGEST PLAYERS IN OUR ELECTIONS—STATE administrators, political parties, the press, voting technology companies—all take it as gospel that the system is as democratic, above board, and as free from malfeasance and error as any major endeavor can be. That credo becomes an excuse to defend a status quo that serves them differently, even as power shifts. Nowhere is this more forcefully seen than with the subject of hacking or electronically stealing votes.

To dismiss hacking as trivial or conspiratorial in 2017 is naive. Yet that's been the line for years—continuing even as Russia got caught stealing DNC and Clinton campaign email, fabricating emails from contractors sent to election officials, and getting inside the Illinois voter registration database.[229] As ex-CIA and NSA Director Michael Hayden told a Heritage Foundation audience in October 2016, hacking adversaries' electronic data is old hat. "I have to admit my definition of what the Russians did is, unfortunately, honorable state espionage," he said. "A foreign intelligence service getting the internal emails of a major political party in a major foreign adversary? Game on. That's what we do. By the way, I would not want to be in an America court of law and be forced to deny I never did anything like that as director of the NSA."[230]

Closer to home, police regularly use hacking technology to intercept and capture online, Wi-Fi, and cell phone-band communications, including devices where the FBI has gone to court to try to keep a lid on sales to departments. These are the same data pathways that voting machines use to report precinct results to central tabulators.[231] More concretely, former state election directors have told me that state motor vehicles databases, which are linked to voter registration databases, are hit routinely—"on a weekly basis"—by overseas hackers, especially from China. There is a false equivalency in the media, which covers GOP claims about voter fraud extensively—even though it barely exists, while ignoring hacking of government systems including those tied to voting and elections. There is an establishment bias that does not want to admit that shortcomings can undermine public trust in elections, instead of proactively addressing them and showing the results can be trusted.

The central problem in this sphere is that there haven't been any serious public examinations, ever, of looking for hacking in voting systems in the immediate aftermath of nationwide elections for the purpose of possibly overturning results. Some academics say it would be impossible to trace malware that fractionally adjusted vote totals at key central tabulation nodes, because these bits of code can erase their electronic footprints. Others say it's still worth looking at. Either way, the voting machinery, with few exceptions, is privatized, protected from scrutiny as trade secrets, and maintained in most counties by contractors. All that feeds the accurate characterizations that it is an unnecessary black box. None of this is reassuring.

Still, I do not first plant myself in the company of those who say nothing else in elections matters if votes can be electronically stolen, because that is ignoring too many other antidemocratic features. It's not an either-or choice. The GOP's attacks on voting are politically shrewd but administratively crude. They take aim at broad swaths of the electorate in a do-everything strategy, because elections are so full of unanticipated twists and turns.

Just as crucially, in more than a dozen years of covering electoral nuts and bolts, I have never seen sufficient proof of major federal elections being stolen electronically. By proof, I mean beyond inferring conclusions from suspicious data points such as exit poll discrepancies, or documenting dubious behavior like Ohio's GOP secretary of state posting the 2004 results on a state website where the RNC had backdoor access to its server; and thus access to what was posted for the media and public. (I helped break that story. George W. Bush came from behind to defeat John Kerry after Ohio's results were frozen for ninety minutes.)[232] To know that the rest of the voting process has been micro-targeted by the GOP for partisan gain but to think that voting machines and tabulators are immune or sacred would be illogical. There may be proof of hacking that fractionally adjusts vote counts, but we just haven't seen it. This fraught terrain set the stage for 2016's recounts.

What the Greens wanted was to verify the vote by having the country's most respected computer scientists look inside the black boxes and share what they found. "History came knocking—who was I to say no to this effort," Stein said. Also, her party had a track record, unlike the Democrats. In Ohio in 2004, the Greens' involvement in the recount led to some structural reforms, at least by then Democratic secretaries of state in Ohio and California. Those states started a national wave of slowly replacing entirely paperless voting systems with hand-marked paper ballots that were electronically scanned, but could be manually examined in recounts and audits. Michigan used paper-based systems in 2016. That's also true for Wisconsin, except for touch screens with printouts for voters with disabilities. Pennsylvania mostly used the oldest entirely paperless systems.[233]

The Greens never came close to looking inside. As Stein summarized in her preinaugural email to donors,

In Michigan, Trump's GOP cronies stopped the recount [after one-third of the state reported] despite—or maybe because of—revelations about major problems with the vote count, particularly in under-resourced black and brown communities. In Wisconsin, although the law was on our side, many low-income communities of color most vulnerable to tampering never got the hand-count needed to verify the vote. But the worst mess was in Pennsylvania, where over 80 percent of voters use touch-screen machines with no tangible paper backup. These paper-less voting machines are so vulnerable to hacking and so difficult to verify that they have been banned in most states."[234]

What emerged from the recount were more partisan attacks that were on par with the most antidemocratic features of the primary season and General Election. In Michigan, Bill Schuette, the Republican attorney general, led the legal charge on Trump's behalf to convince its courts to stop the recount, because, among other arguments, Stein had no real chance of winning. What was overlooked in that argument was the most easily answered question surrounding the state with the closest margin between Clinton and Trump—why did seventy-five thousand ballots lack presidential votes? Most explanations were deeply unsatisfying, amounting to, as Philip Bump wrote in the *Washington Post* in December, "It happens." He reported that nationally, 1.7 million people in thirty-three states cast no presidential vote. Michigan was in the bottom third of states, percentage-wise.[235] What Bump and many mainstream media reporters never argued was that a hand recount of paper ballots, not just running them through high-speed scanners, would not just reveal whether those ballots missed votes. It would reveal where Trump's base was, where people who skipped voting lived, and other important facts that would have helped the country move forward.

The highest-profile snafus that emerged in Michigan's brief recount were in Detroit. There, it became apparent that the city's elections were a mess. More than half the precincts were barred from the recount because the number of ballots inside tabulator bins did not match the number of voters written on the outside of those bins by poll workers.

As Jan BenDor, the Michigan Election Reform Alliance's statewide coordinator, noted at the time, the state has a 1954 law giving full power to local officials to look at all the ballots in recounts. But state election officials, pressured by Republicans in constitutional offices, countered that a 1979 administrative rule prevented them from doing so. Many progressives and civil rights attorneys saw that decision as institutional racism, treating Detroit separately and unequally.[236] When Secretary of State Ruth Johnson published a report on Detroit's election woes in 2017, the incongruities were mostly blamed on poll workers. While their incompetence may have been real, just as local Iowans and Nevadans running Democratic Party presidential caucuses botched those contests, that explanation—beyond reassigning blame— underscores the system is not up to its assigned task.

Other postelection analyses noted additional institutional bar- riers in Michigan. The affidavit developed by state Election Director Chris Thomas—where people lacking ID or not listed in precinct poll books swore they were registered voters and received a regular bal- lot—was not promoted by poll workers, according to a summer 2017 report by Miles Rapoport, the former Connecticut secretary of state and Democrat, who was president of Demos and Common Cause. He also wrote, "Michigan is another Crosscheck state, where five hundred thousand 'potential duplicates' were found, and at least fifty-five thou- sand voters were taken off the rolls as a result."[237]

In neighboring Wisconsin, different obstacles emerged in a state that until recently had the best nonpartisan election overseers in the country, a bipartisan panel of retired state judges known as the Government Accountability Board. However, Republican Gov. Scott Walker and a GOP-majority legislature retired that panel, among other anti-voter laws they passed, and raised the statewide recount filing fee from about $18,000 to $3.5 million. After Stein's campaign paid up, the newly created Wisconsin Elections Commission said counties could run the paper ballots through high-speed scanners instead of recount- ing them by hand.

That decision flustered the Greens' intent of a verifiable recount and led them to sue. Their court affidavits from computer scientists, such as from University of California Berkeley computing and mathematics professor Philip B. Stark, noted the 22,525-vote difference between Clinton and Trump was 0.776 percent of the 2.9 million votes cast. That margin, percentage-wise, is less than the standard error rates of high-speed scanners, he said.[238] Dane County Circuit Judge Valerie Bailey-Rihn ruled that even though a hand recount was preferable, she could not force counties to do that. As a result, Wisconsin's most populous counties—Milwaukee (440,000 presidential votes), Waukesha (237,000 votes), Brown (129,000 votes), and Racine (94,000 votes)—all rescanned their ballots, flouting best practices to verify the vote.

Activists watching the state's hand recounts tallied nearly eighteen thousand votes that were incorrectly scanned on November 8. But when it was all over, officials said that Trump had increased his victory margin by about four hundred votes—prompting media yawns and ridicule of the Greens. Meanwhile, Arizona-based activist John Brakey noticed and confirmed, contrary to many statements by officials, that one of the most commonly used voting machines in Wisconsin and nationally, ES&S model DS200, used cell phone modems to transmit precinct results to central tabulators. That potential hacking pathway cast doubts on the results, Brakey said. Legal discovery by the Greens also revealed the state did not require the contractors who maintained and programmed the voting machines to take extra security steps. Despite these windows into Wisconsin's less-than-ideal infrastructure, it was the only state to complete a recount, and no new numbers emerged to change the result.

The state that received the least attention in the recount, Pennsylvania, was the most antidemocratic. "The primary reason Pennsylvania was recounted was to take a close forensic look at the electronic voting machines, since the state is not designed to be recounted," wrote Bob Fitrakis, an Ohio-based attorney and longtime legal advisor to the Greens on elections, in the *Columbus Free Press*, where he is editor and publisher.[239] Local election integrity activists like Dr. Michelle Zuckerman-Parker, a medical researcher in Allegheny County, where Pittsburgh is located, typified the volunteers who tried to help the Greens. She documented inconsistencies among "data values" in the county and state systems managing voter rolls and tabulating votes, and was hoping a recount might spotlight these lapses.[240] While that was the agenda of computer scientists and election integrity activists, the Greens' grassroots supporters faced an insurmountable task on the ground: submitting recount petitions and notarized affidavits from three voters in each of the state's 9,158 precincts and laying out $450,000 in filing fees.

As Jonathan S. Abady, the lead lawyer for the Greens' legal team wrote to Attorney General Loretta Lynch on December 23, 2016, about Pennsylvania, "This year, voters who sought to confirm that their votes had been accurately recorded by requesting recounts were thwarted by a byzantine, unworkable, legal regime." County boards conducting official vote counts don't disclose when they've finished, Abady noted, which is supposed to trigger a narrow recount filing window. "Two of the state's largest counties (Allegheny and Delaware) admitted in court that their boards of elections do not comply with the legally mandated process for completing the count. Not even the state's top election officials knew when the various counties had finished counting the vote. . ."[241]

Abady didn't stop there. He noted how one state court demanded a $1 million bond from ordinary voters filing recount petitions. He said that the need for recounts was prompted by "at least two types of vulnerabilities: susceptibility to malicious interference and poor performance." Turning to other recount states, Abady cited eighty-seven broken machines "in Detroit alone." He noted Halderman "has personally hacked into several voting machines as part of a research study, including the optical scan model used in Michigan." Abady wrote, "FBI Director James Comey's sworn testimony to Congress that no election machines are ever connected to the internet . . . is inaccurate," citing the new "ES&S DS200 model is in broad use in approximately twenty-five states." He concluded, "The United States should investigate these irregularities and vulnerabilities," adding the country needed "paper ballot-based systems," "automatic audits, for every election," and "adequate funding of our election system to maintain voting machines and train election staff."[242]

Needless to say, neither the federal government, nor the Clinton campaign, nor Pennsylvania's Democratic executive branch leadership including Secretary of the Commonwealth Pedro Cortes, nor its state judiciary bothered to reply to the substance of the Greens' concerns. As Fitrakis wrote in early January, "U.S. District Judge Paul Diamond states that suspicion of a hacked election in the Quaker State 'borders on the irrational.' In prohibiting a presidential recount, Diamond held that there was 'no credible evidence that any "hack" occurred and compelling evidence that Pennsylvania's voting system was not in any way compromised.' Diamond's ruling came a day after the *Washington Post* claimed that a secret CIA report found the Russians interfering in the US election electronically in order to hurt Clinton and aid Trump."[243]

Still, many voting rights attorneys, even those who have led the fights against GOP anti-voter laws, are more than reluctant to say administrative mistakes and misdeeds should be subject to criminal penalties. They fall under the "bad policy" umbrella, which lawsuits can challenge and legislatures can rectify, these lawyers explain, rather than statutory crimes such as explicit voter intimidation and specific Voting Rights Act violations.[244] (While I've known and respected these lawyers for many years, I can only wonder aloud if the betrayal by our voting system of American democracy requires its custodians to be held to higher standards and penalties—even if they will be deeply opposed by most public officials.)

By early fall 2017, when this book is being finished, we know a lot more about what Russia did and didn't do. When Trump finally met Vladimir Putin at a July G-20 meeting in Germany, both perfectly played the part of any longtime politico who never would admit to anything that would undermine their power. They agreed that Russia didn't interfere in the election or collude with the Trump campaign. (The Justice Department's Special Counsel, former FBI director Robert Mueller, may have more to say about that narrative.) Russia clearly interfered and had influence, said Timothy Snyder, a Yale historian of early twentieth-century authoritarian regimes—including the Soviet Union. In a mid-June speech, Snyder explained the Russians didn't need to tinker with voting machinery, even though they were probing those systems, because they found a much more effective way to influence voters: inundate them with propaganda on social media.[245]

Snyder said we know that Russians hacked the DNC and Clinton campaign emails before spring and summer 2016. Trump also invited them to do more of it while campaigning, he noted. (That was before disclosures in 2017 congressional testimony that dozens of states were targeted, and the early June publication by TheIntercept.com of a National Security Agency document with more details, such as fake emails sent by Russia to election vendors and local offices. Notably, most actions cited by the NSA were after October 27, 2016, long after voter registration had closed in Florida, Georgia, Michigan, Nevada, North Carolina, Ohio, Pennsylvania, and Virginia.[246])

Snyder explained that Russia didn't have to focus on voting machinery because they had a bigger, more effective strategy. As Bloomberg's Joshua Green and Sasha Issenberg reported in late October 2016, the campaign's social media operation targeted Clinton supporters on Facebook and Twitter with negative messaging to discourage them from voting for her.[247] These weren't just traditional political ads that had been diverted online, but as Facebook said in its April 2017 report, "Social media accounts and pages were created to amplify news accounts of and direct people to the stolen data. From there, organic proliferation of the messaging and data through authentic peer groups and networks was inevitable."[248] In other words, Trump's campaign bombarded swing-state Democrats with political ads and fake news, some of which were based on information stolen in Russian hacks of the DNC and Clinton campaign.[249]

"The main element of the Russian intervention in the election had to do with gathering political data about tens of millions of Americans, and then using Facebook and other platforms to target fake news to people who were regarded as susceptible, especially in the last weeks before the election, which probably determined the outcome in critical states that were targeted," Snyder said. "This isn't to say that there aren't other reasons, and in my view, good reasons, why people could vote for Mr. Trump. It isn't to say that Hillary Clinton ran a wonderful campaign either. It's just to say that in a very close election, that probably made the difference."[250]

If Snyder is correct, Russia more than learned the lessons of the Republican playbook. They looked at 2016's political landscape and found vulnerabilities where targeted interventions could scale. Why mess with Michigan's 1,600 local election jurisdictions or Wisconsin's 1,850 election jurisdictions, and their respective computer systems, when they could use social media to target those states' voters with provocative propagandistic messaging? That tactic was akin to the "honorable state espionage" cited by former CIA and NSA Director Hayden in his October 2016 speech at the Heritage Foundation.[251] Strategically, this is no different than any other negative political advertising campaign seeking to discourage the opposing side's voters. Instead of deluging voters with attack-dog mailings, they used social media platforms like Facebook and promoted propagandistic stories in American right-wing media that drew on information obtained by Russia's hacking of Democrats.

But let's step back and grasp the big picture. Whether extreme partisan redistricting, newly restrictive voter ID requirements, paper proof of citizenship requirements, limiting early voting opportunities, moving polling places, repealing Election Day registration, there is a long list of Republican strategies that shave points off of likely turnout by Democratic voting blocs. These tactics are all politically shrewd *because* they are administratively crude. They take aim widely at multitudes and await the consequences. It appears that Russia followed this same template.

Meanwhile, research since the election addressed some of the anomalies cited by Bonifaz on the eve of the recounts. A study by the University of Michigan's Walter Mebane Jr., a professor of political science and statistics, and Matthew Bernhard, a PhD computer science scholar, examined the recount data in Michigan and Wisconsin to see if the different voting technologies—ink-marked paper ballots versus electronic touch screens—treated Clinton and Trump differently. "Presumably, if there had been a hack to benefit or harm one candidate, the voting machines would have systematically under- or over-counted one candidate's ballots more than the other," they wrote for the *Washington Post*'s "Monkey Cage" blog in early June 2017. "That didn't happen."[252]

"Our analysis assumes that the recount, when done by hand, accurately counted the votes," they said, agreeing with the Greens' methodology. "In brief, we find no evidence that the voting technology favored one candidate more than the other . . . The tests uncovered nothing suspicious. That supports a conclusion that voting machines themselves were not hacked."

That analysis put to rest one concern that emerged immediately after the election. However, it didn't suggest that electronic voting machines weren't vulnerable. Hackers attending the DEF CON25 conference in July 2017 in Las Vegas "claimed to have found major vulnerabilities or claimed to have breached every voting machine and system present," wrote Lulu Freisdat, who videotaped their effort. She reported the breached systems included "the Sequoia AVC Edge, currently in use in thirteen states and the AccuVote TSX, in use in nineteen states."[253] Hackers also took "complete control of an e-poll book" and scrambled their files, she said, noting these hacks took from a few minutes to a few hours—another metric about our elections.

But Mebane and Bernhard's analysis of the Greens' recount had a bombshell—though not enough to unseat Trump. They didn't find evidence of hacking, but they did find something else that could have changed the result. "We ran into a different problem in Michigan: only a subset of precincts were recounted," they said. "Serious problems have been documented in Detroit that potentially could have changed the outcome in the state."[254]

Rapoport, too, believed that the aborted recount, reports of spoiled ballots in Detroit, and partisan voter purges facilitated by Crosscheck's lousy data all "had a cumulative impact that likely exceeded Trump's 11,000-vote margin."[255]

Another postelection study, led by Professor Kenneth R. Mayer of the University of Wisconsin-Madison, found that Wisconsin's strict voter ID law discouraged 16,800 voters from casting ballots in the state's two most populous counties. Those suppressed votes were equal to 11.2 percent of those counties' electorate, leading many observers to conclude that, statewide, the voter ID law could have led to Trump's nearly 23,000 vote victory.[256]

So Clinton should have won Michigan and Wisconsin, but that still wasn't enough to win the presidency.

THE ELECTORAL COLLEGE

THE RECOUNTS EXPOSED MORE UNSAVORY FEATURES of American elections. Yet, as has been the case for years, election officials grudgingly accepted these slights as an inevitable part of the process. The recount's shortcomings joined the list of Election Day impediments compiled by groups like the League of Women Voters, whose post-2016 Wisconsin report cited many incidents of voters being shuffled between polls, confusion over voter ID requirements, and provisional ballots. In a state with millions voting however, hundreds of random victims were seen as an unfortunate but not outcome-changing cost to be tolerated.

Nonetheless, the cumulative toll of a presidential campaign that was widely called one of the "worst ever" kept prompting people to look for a final way to stop Trump. As the recounts churned along, the Republican Party's members of their state Electoral College prepared to meet in their Capitol buildings to ratify the presidential results. That led to an effort by a group called the Hamilton Electors, named after Alexander Hamilton, who argued that the GOP's almost-final gatekeepers owed it to their country to reject Trump and pick someone else.

"I am asked to cast a vote on Dec. 19 for someone who shows daily he is not qualified for the office," wrote Christopher Suprun, a Texas paramedic and Republican elector, for *The New York Times'* opinion page. "The election of the next president is not yet a done deal.

Presidential electors have the legal right and constitutional duty to vote their conscience. I believe electors should unify behind a Republican alternative."[257]

Suprum's Electoral College brethren did not respond to his call to arms. In fact, the only electors to reject their party's nominee were a few Democrats who abandoned Clinton. That left one final possibility, urging members of Congress to reject the Electoral College's vote for ratification in its joint session in early January. The last time members of both chambers rose to block the ratification was in 2005. That January, Ohio's Rep. Stephanie Tubbs-Jones and California's Sen. Barbara Boxer forced the House and the Senate to return to their chambers for a two-hour debate, where they heard now-familiar complaints about voter suppression. As in 2005, civil rights activists urged the Congressional Black Caucus to take the lead.

"We are writing to you as a member of the Black Caucus to ask you to file an objection before January 6, 2017, when you and your colleagues reconvene to count and authenticate the ill-gotten votes that some electors cast for Donald Trump," Ruby Sales, Amy Billingsley, and Ann Massaro wrote. "Whether you realize it or not, there is another powder keg that is percolating in Black, Brown, and progressive communities who voted in large numbers for Secretary Clinton only to have their votes stolen and disregarded not only by Republicans but seemingly by Democrats."[258]

Their letter cited the seventy-five thousand Michigan ballots lacking votes for president, the "massive non-count of ballots in Milwaukee [that] doubtless contain the tally that defeated Mr. Trump," and "missing tally from communities of color" in Pennsylvania, among anti-voter actions. Their conviction and determination was laudable, but some facts were not on their side such as how some sixty thousand fewer voters turned out in Milwaukee compared to 2012, and how it was virtually impossible to know what was or wasn't missing in Pennsylvania because its voting machinery was almost all paperless, including in Philadelphia and Pittsburgh.

Just days before Congress was to convene, emergency petitions were filed at the Supreme Court. Jerroll M. Sanders, a Missouri activist, argued the election should be voided because federal officeholders were elected by a foreign power—Russia. That went nowhere. In the meantime, as a handful of House Democrats said they would contest the ratification, Ryan Clayton, with the group Americans Take Action, released a thousand-page report from a team of lawyers and law students that claimed fifty Republican members of the Electoral College were illegally seated.[259]

This should have been a bombshell. The "Electoral Vote Objection Package" said sixteen GOP electors lived outside of the congressional districts they purportedly represented, and thirty-four more Republican electors were dual officeholders in states that barred elected officials from holding more than one office. Being an Electoral College member, however brief the term, was an elected office. "Ironically, Florida Attorney General Pam Bondi, who has issued a number of Advisory Legal Opinions on dual-officeholding, was a presidential elector," their executive summary said. "Joe Negron, who also cast an electoral vote, is currently President of the Florida Senate."

The findings by Clayton's team were a stunning final example of a party that is willing to ignore or revise the rules of voting in an endless pursuit of power. When a few progressive House members rose to challenge the Electoral College certification, they barely got to say more than a sound bite beyond the formalities. (Had their challenge succeeded, the selection of the president would have gone to the House. It didn't get that far.)

With Vice President Joe Biden presiding, Massachusetts Rep. James McGovern rose. "I object to the certificate from the state of Alabama on the grounds that the electoral votes were not under all of the known circumstances regularly given and the electors were not lawfully certified, especially given the confirmed and illegal activities engaged in by the Government of Russia that were designed to interfere with our election and widespread violations of the Voting Rights

Act that unlawfully suppressed thousands of votes in the state of Alabama."

"Is the objection in writing and signed not only by a Member of the House but also by a Senator?" Biden replied.

"The objection is in writing and is signed by a Member of the House of Representatives but not yet by a Member of the United States Senate," McGovern countered.

"In that case, the objection cannot be entertained," Biden said.[260]

And so it went. Maryland's Jamie Raskin, Washington's Pramila Jayapal, California's Barbara Lee, and Texas' Shiela Jackson Lee all rose to file objections and were gaveled down. California's Maxine Waters rose, saying, "I wish to ask: is there one United States Senator who will join me in this letter of objection?"

None replied.

The certification continued with one more attempted objection by Arizona's Raoul Grijalva.

But Biden cut him off, saying, "There is no debate in the joint session . . . Is there a signature from a Senator?" He replied no, prompting Jackson Lee to rise again, saying she objected to North Carolina's certification, "because of the massive voter suppression and the closing of voting, massive suppression that occurred from African-American—" Tersely, Biden gaveled her down. "The tellers will continue the count."

In her extension of remarks that were added to the Congressional Record, Jackson Lee recounted the election's arc. Historians will "surely record that the 2016 campaign was one for the ages," she wrote. Clinton was widely considered "the most qualified person ever nominated for the office." Trump "is the first person to gain an Electoral College majority with no experience whatsoever in elective or appointive governmental office or public service." It was the "first time in history that a Director of the Federal Bureau of Investigation had ever injected himself and his agency" into the race. It was "the first American presidential election that the Intelligence Community has confirmed was the subject of cyberattacks and other subversive activities of entities allied with the Government of Russia." She tried to strike a bright note, saying, "Hillary Clinton received more votes for president than any person in history not named Barack Obama, which means the two greatest vote getters in American political history are an African-American male and white female, which is a testament to how far America has traveled on the path to equality."[261]

But then Jackson Lee returned to brass tacks. "A switch of less than eighty thousand votes in just three states—Pennsylvania, Michigan, and Wisconsin—would have secured an Electoral College majority for Hillary Clinton," she said, but "that fact is of little consolation and practical consequence to the situation and task now before us." She ended, "There is compelling evidence that activities engaged in by state officials violated the Voting Rights Act of 1965 and disenfranchised thousands of voters and resulted in the unlawful certification of electors . . . The fate of our democracy is at stake."

Brave words, but not one senator would sign her letters of objection to voting in North Carolina, Pennsylvania, and Wisconsin. Democracy Spring activists shouted protests from the gallery and were arrested. The presidential election was officially over. The following week, Bret Sablosky, a paralegal who moved to Washington to block Trump, filed a federal court motion to postpone the inauguration. "The popular vote plurality is the only Constitutional method of electing the President and Vice President," he argued, saying the Electoral College was an unconstitutional under slavery-ending amendments.

His lawsuit was dismissed.

AFTERWORD

As I write almost a year into Trump's presidency, the voting rights pendulum is heading back to the dark side. The forces in American politics that want to stop all eligible citizens from voting are newly empowered. States with supermajority red legislatures are not just trying to suppress Democratic voters, but preempting the very issues that blue voters and municipalities can vote on.[262] These threats to American democracy and representative government pose profound questions that transcend not only the future of the parties, but what it means to be citizens now and in the future.

The Republican war on voting has continued, taking its cues from President Trump. Even before his swearing in, he told congressional leaders that between three and five million illegal votes were cast for Clinton to deny him a popular vote majority.[263] Never mind that the AP found Gregg Phillips, the source for Trump's false claim, "was registered to vote in multiple states in the 2016 election."[264] That underscores, yet again, that all the GOP noise about policing the vote is as hypocritical as it is fake. The press may expose Trump's tweets as lies, but that has not stopped top White House aides from repeating them.

National Policy Director Stephen Miller echoed Trump by telling a national TV audience that he only lost New Hampshire because illegal voters were bused in from Massachusetts. Rep. Steve, R-Iowa, told another national audience it was plausible. Bill Gardner, who has been New Hampshire's secretary of state since 1976, said there was no proof. Tom Rath, the state's former attorney general and a Republican said that it was "shameful to spread these fantasies."[265] Even Trump's first campaign manager, Corey Lewandoski, who lives near the border, said he didn't see any buses.[266]

But that propaganda circus is typical of Trump and obscures more serious GOP actions. As *Washington Post* political reporter Dan Balz noted about Trump's presidential-size illegal voter claim, "There is no benign explanation . . . It is either a deliberate attempt to undermine faith in the democratic process, an exhortation to those who favor new restrictions on access to the ballot box, or the worrisome trait of someone with immense power willing to make wild statements without any credible evidence."[267]

All of the above are true. But what has emerged since Trump took office is especially Balz's second prospect, which does not bode well for American democracy. The larger stakes are what is happening under this administration to further unwind representative government.

Trump has empowered vote suppressors to transform the Department of Justice, whose Civil Rights Division just celebrated its sixtieth anniversary. The Attorney General, Jeff Sessions, began his career prosecuting one of Dr. Martin Luther King's associates for voter fraud.[268] By late February, the Department said it would not pursue its lawsuit against Texas's voter ID law, which it had been fighting for the past several years.[269] As a *Huffington Post* headline succinctly observed, "Obama's DOJ Fought Texas Voter ID Law. Trump's New Civil Rights Chief Offered Tips On Writing It."[270]

The voter suppressors were just getting going. At the end of March, two dozen conservative activists and lawyers, including men who oversaw the DOJ's voter fraud investigations during George W. Bush's administration, wrote an unsolicited letter[271] to Sessions. They presented a classic white supremacist agenda: back off laws protective of minority voters and start pressuring states to aggressively purge their voter lists.

"We have witnessed longstanding conventions held from the mid-20th century prove outmoded in recent years and discovered new fronts in need of protection where civil rights are concerned—with particular respect to voting," said the letter signed by Kansas Secretary of State Kris Kobach, The Heritage Foundation's Hans von Spakovsky, and the Public Interest Legal Foundation's J. Christian Adams, among others.[272]

In early May, Trump appointed these three men to a Presidential Advisory Commission on Election Integrity, where Kobach is vice-chair. (Vice President Mike Pence is the titular chair.)[273] While their initial meetings were held in secret, the March letter to Sessions laid out their agenda. They seek a "return to race-neutral Voting Rights Act enforcement," "an end to politically driven pursuits against state photo voter identification requirements, citizenship verification in voter registration, and common-sense adjustments to early voting periods," and "return to enforcing Section 8" of the NVRA, which governs voter purges. They ended, "The American electorate is crying out to see protections against political enforcement of the law."[274]

These missives and presidential missions are the opening moves in the next round of an ugly fight over who gets to vote in America and how arduous that process will be. This especially is the case in states that have been most heavily gerrymandered and are key to control of the House (and include presidential swing states). These are states like Michigan, Wisconsin, Pennsylvania, North Carolina, Ohio, Virginia, Florida, Georgia, and Texas.

One of Kobach's first tactics has been to demand all fifty states turn over their voter files, including lists of inactive voters and confidential data like Social Security numbers.[275] While progressives, Democrats, civil rights groups, and others have loudly protested and sought to defy Kobach's commission, some election experts who have watched him for years believe that this data grab is a giant bait and switch. (Kobach has not said why the commission is seeking the statewide voter data or what it will do with it.)

Kobach knows most states can't meet his deadline even if they wanted to, Michael McDonald, a University of Florida associate professor specializing in American elections, tweeted after Kobach's letter became public.[276] That's because, among other things, many states are not authorized by legislatures to share everything he wants. Knowing that is likely to be the case positions him and Trump to say that states are hiding evidence of voter fraud. That's exactly what Trump tweeted on July 1, "Numerous states are refusing to give information to the very distinguished VOTER FRAUD PANEL. What are they trying to hide?"[277]

By late July, seven lawsuits had been filed against the commission. Dozens of states were saying they would only partly comply and some top state election officials openly said they didn't trust Kobach. At the panel's first public meeting, Trump stopped by and said, "one has to wonder what they are worried about," referring to recalcitrant states. And then the panel's discussion, chaired by Kobach and dominated by von Spakovsky, suggested using known problematic government databases to vet (and erroneously reject) voter applications.[278]

Those records included the US Department of Homeland Security's incomplete citizenship database—which Florida Republicans previously sought to use. Von Spakovsky also wanted jury duty records, to see if people who said they were noncitizens to avoid jury duty were registered voters. He also wanted state tax records to see if someone had registered to vote at a business address instead of a home address. The panel also wanted a list of elections from across the country where the winner was decided by single-digit margins.[279]

These demands, especially from von Spakovsky, did not surprise election lawyers who favor expanding the franchise. Von Spakovsky's role during the Bush administration of undermining the Justice Department's pro-voting rights mission was widely documented, starting with his false and outsized claims about voter fraud. As Rick Hasen, an election law expert at the University of California at Irvine blogged in late June 2017, "The appointment is a big middle finger from the president to those who are serious about fixing problems with our elections."[280]

All of this points to fabricating a pretext for newly restrictive federal anti-voter legislation—or red states with super majorities to further complicate the process of voting. Recall there is no nationwide federal database for voter fraud, or for citizenship—a useful absence that allows Republicans to say the process must be better policed; and then using imprecise methodologies that disproportionately target blue voting blocs.

More potentially insidious, on the same day that Kobach sent his letter seeking state voter files and related data, the DOJ's Voting Section also sent the same states a demand letter on a parallel fishing expedition. It asked all the states to provide everything they use—"all statutes, regulations, written guidance, internal policies, or database use manuals that set out the procedures"—relating to the "list maintenance provisions" of the National Voter Registration Act (NVRA) and Help America Vote Act (HAVA).[281] Their letter said nothing about expanding registration, only about removing previously registered voters who may have moved, died, been convicted of a felony, or were on inactive voter lists. It doesn't take much to see where this is going. Trump's commission and DOJ's Voting Section are following the template laid out in the late March 2017 letter from longtime GOP vote suppressors, including those who led the Bush administration's voter fraud inquests.[282]

What may happen is that Kobach and company will hold off issuing any report until 2018, at the earliest. That's because the Supreme Court's fall 2017 term contains two big voting cases, where its right-wing majority might issue rulings enshrining key pieces of the GOP's anti-voter playbook. (Early in 2018 is also when state legislatures reconvene, and where red states could fast-track any recommendations before the 2018 elections.)

The first case coming before the Court, from Ohio, concerns how soon infrequent voters can be purged under the NVRA.[283] The law has an ambiguity that Republicans identified and are trying to exploit. It lays out a four-year timetable for voter purges, but also says that no one can be removed for being an infrequent voter, an apparent contradiction. Georgia's GOP Secretary of State Brain Kemp, now running for governor—like Kansas' Kobach—filed a brief on behalf of a dozen red states urging the court take the case. In August 2017, Trump's Justice Department filed a brief supporting Ohio's GOP-led purge, reversing the DOJ's stance taken during the Obama administration.[284]

The second case is from Wisconsin on whether extreme partisan redistricting is legal.[285] More than a decade ago, Justice Anthony Kennedy wrote an opinion suggesting the Court would like to see a standard for assessing when partisan gerrymanders are so extreme they become unconstitutionally antidemocratic. Law professors have created a metric based on "wasted votes" using Wisconsin as an example. But in the Supreme Court's late May ruling about illegal racial gerrymandering in North Carolina, Kennedy signed a dissent suggesting he may have changed his mind about extreme redistricting. The dissenters said such hyper-partisanship was distasteful but part of human nature and the political process. The ruling in these cases will determine the electoral playing field for years to come.

Meanwhile, despite populist expectations among Democrats that they can retake the House in 2018, there are other signs the national landscape is tightening in antidemocratic ways. Looking at 2016's results, REDMAP states continued to see red supermajorities elected to their House delegations and state legislatures. Extreme redistricting is to blame for the noncompetitive races that produced the political landscapes in these states and Congress, Daley reiterated in a post-2016 epilogue to his book, *Ratf**ked*.[286] After the 2016 election, the GOP held sixty-nine of the niety-nine state legislative chambers. There is little reason to think Republican supermajority states will see Democratic takeovers in 2018 or 2020—the year before their legislatures draw political maps lasting for the 2020s, he said. That likelihood makes 2018's governor races in states where Republican incumbents face term limits—such as Florida, Michigan, Ohio, and Georgia—the most important races if the GOP's lock is to be broken. Only Democratic governors can veto the bad maps that likely will be drawn in 2021.

Meanwhile, when it comes to retaking the US House, 2016's results showed the 2011 gerrymander continues to hold. Even though Republican candidates received 1.2 percent more votes nationwide, they ended up with 10.8 percent more seats. What most Democrats don't grasp looking at 2018 is how steep the climb back into power is. As Daley said in July 2017, Democrats have only flipped one seat from red to blue in five key states since 2011's maps—in Michigan, Ohio, Pennsylvania, Wisconsin, and Virginia. That seat was in Virginia, after a court ruled it had been an illegal race-based gerrymander. When Democrats say they are looking at taking the twenty-three GOP seats in House districts where Clinton defeated Trump—they need twenty-four to regain a majority—Daley countered that's not a reassuring strategy. They need to compete in fifty competitive races, he said, and he doesn't see that taking shape.[287]

There are other ominous trends. One of the biggest trends following red super majorities is not merely restricting the process of voting, but going further to restrict what citizens locally vote on. This trend has the clunky name of preemption, but is very serious.[288] In the most gerrymandered states, there are schisms between red-run legislatures and blue-run cities, which have passed all kinds of progressive laws— from higher minimum wages, to banning natural gas hydraulic fracturing, to being sanctuaries for immigrants, to taxing soda and tobacco, to banning guns in public, and more. Red legislatures have responded with new statewide laws to reverse and ban local initiatives. The GOP, which once venerated local control, are now more than willing to preempt what entire populations can vote on. Segregating voters via extreme redistricting and blocking access to the polls is antidemocratic enough. But censoring what citizens can vote on is astounding.

What Democrats, progressives, and independents must realize, whether they are focusing on the House in 2018 or state legislatures, are

the structural disadvantages they face. The GOP, in the most heavily gerrymandered districts, has a 6–8 percentage point starting line advantage.
These are states where red legislatures have kept passing stricter voter
ID laws—which shave off another 2–3 points in the November election,
and much more in primaries among blacks, Asians, and Latinos. These
states may follow Kobach's lead and impose new documented proof of
citizenship requirements for registrants, which 7 percent of the public
lacks. These tactics are followed by other anti-voter moves, from limiting
early voting options to ending Election Day registration.

But by summer 2017, it was not clear the GOP's structural advantages were understood. Few apart from the Democratic Governors
Association talk about the importance of upcoming governors' races,
compared to retaking the House. Meanwhile, other Republican gambits in order to preserve their power are surfacing and have to be taken
seriously.

When ALEC, the right-wing American Legislative Exchange
Council, met in July 2017, it discussed two structural reforms to create
a permanent Republican majority. The first was restoring the appointment of US Senators by state legislatures by repealing the Seventeenth
Amendment. (After November 2016, the GOP held both chambers in
thirty-two states, which, if such a repeal were law, would mean they
would have sixty-four senators.) As far-fetched as that sounds, ALEC
has been pushing red states to pass legislation calling for a federal
Article Five constitutional convention, where such a proposal could be
raised. So far, twenty-seven states out of the thirty-four states needed
have passed resolutions for that convention.

A more likely near-term threat is gerrymandering the Electoral
College. Republicans could do that by replacing the statewide winner-
take-all system with awarding delegates by House district. If that were
law in Virginia, where a bill was introduced but did not pass in 2017, the
state's eleven Electoral College votes would not have gone to Clinton;
Trump carried six of its House districts.[289] Legislation to do that was
proposed in a few states in early 2017, but did not go anywhere.

Too few people pay attention to these potential power grabs. But they would continue what Republicans have done this decade. They have transformed voting to such a degree that it has subverted our democracy. There's no indication they intend to reverse course and put representative government before their partisan power. If anything, the opposite is true. They are betraying the citizenry by hijacking voting at key nodes across the process.

Every month into Trump's presidency underscores the antidemocratic result: a political party representing a minority keeps pushing an authoritarian regime of oligarchy, plutocracy, and theocracy. The vast majority of citizens don't support Trump or the GOP's agenda, yet they are witnessing their government being taken from them. The stakes for the country are bigger than which party, or party factions, win or lose. If voting is rendered meaningless, representative government will disintegrate and the American experiment will end.

The only way to stop this trajectory is to understand what's taking place and dismantle the structural advantages the Republicans built into the voting process. This book has tried to describe the antidemocratic features of the 2016 election, which is the latest manifestation of that landscape. It's possible to quantify these features with metrics that didn't exist a decade ago. Understanding what is impeding an increasingly diverse citizenry from voting to elect a representative government is the first step in countering the assault on our democracy.

On the Democratic side of the aisle, the party that is the champion of voting rights must step up to the moral challenge to representative government. The party loses its moral authority when it continues to have features like its superdelegate system, a national apparatus that takes sides in presidential nominating contests, registration deadlines and rules that prevent independents from voting in its primaries, as well as presidential caucuses that are manned by inept volunteers. Party loyalists need to stop defending the indefensible and side with all voters.

But the hurdles posed by Republicans are far more serious, insidious, and embedded in law. We have seen enough of the GOP playbook to do more than object. We know how restrictive voter ID laws impact voter turnout, especially along racial lines. We know about the extreme gerrymandering. We know about possibly replacing a legal oath by signature on voter registration forms with paper proof of citizenship. We also know vast numbers of Republicans believe the myth of voter fraud and support policing the vote. We also know half of Republicans would accept a political coup—postponing the 2020 election if Trump and Congress called for that, according to an August poll by the *Washington Post*. (Even if the US Constitution's Twentieth Amendment sets terms of office with expiration dates.)[290]

But we can quantify how much of the electorate the GOP seeks to preempt. This matters because when people start arguing about elections, the first thing that is lost is magnitude and scale: what is the possible or real impact on voters? Arguing about elections is filled with false equivalencies, hyped impacts, distortions, and prejudice. The Republicans cite one-in-a-million incidents as reasons to pass state laws affecting millions of voters. Citizens who want fair and accountable elections, and representative government, need to push back wisely, and know what matters most.

They need to realize the stakes and yet not give up hope. Nobody knows where the Trump-Russia probes will go. Nor if disgusted voters will turn out in such large numbers in 2018 that they will swamp the GOP's ten-point starting line advantage in a wave sweeping them from office. Meanwhile, voters should look at all possible ways to take back this process. Extreme redistricting is increasingly in the news, with maverick Republicans like former California governor Arnold Schwarzenegger saying backroom mapmakers need to be replaced by citizens' commissions. The political class needs to know the public has their number.

One such glimmer of hope emerged from the Greens' recount. Unlike most of this book, it concerned voting's finish line: verifying the count. John Brakey, the election transparency activist, pointed to a development that can lead to citizen-led verifiable vote counts, even with electronic voting machines. It's a humble prospect, but in the right direction.

"In an 'ah-ha' moment, Election Integrity investigators realized that 40 percent of the voting machines presently in use have the built-in ability to transparently verify reported election results RIGHT NOW," he wrote for a presentation at the Left Forum in New York City in June 2017.[291] "The machines that are used to count hand-marked paper ballots are rapidly being replaced with technology that uses digital imagery to count scanned ballot images. At the current rate, by the next presidential election, approximately 85 percent of the country will generate scanned ballot images."

Brakey envisions crowd-sourcing recounts and audits using images of marked ballots. It's not entirely magical thinking, when you consider NASA puts online telescope images of distant galaxies so thousands of volunteers parse them to find new stars.[292] Of course, it would be better if American elections were held using ink-marked paper ballots that were openly counted and rigorously audited. Brakey believes in the better angels of democracy. But he also knows who and what he's fighting. Many local election officials do not want citizens to pore over ballots to see if their votes have been accurately counted.

Such is the state of our elections in 2018. The closer you look, the more antidemocratic features emerge. Right now, American democracy is in deep trouble. Anything that restores rights of voters and engages citizens cannot be overlooked. Nothing less than the nation's future, the majority voices of citizens, and our future, is at stake.

ACKNOWLEDGMENTS

THE OBSERVATIONS AND CONCLUSIONS PRESENTED IN this book span more than a decade of being a journalist who was given the opportunity to interview, observe, collaborate with, and learn from scores of people with different roles in the voting sphere. These include journalists, lawyers, activists, scholars, foundation officials, candidates, campaign workers, and many authors I have not met but whose work I've read for years. As Bill Moyers said, journalists are beachcombers on the shores of other people's wisdom. That is the case here.

This book began with an unexpected call from John Bonifaz, a voting-rights attorney I met in the 1990s, whose work has crossed my path over the decades. My coverage at AlterNet of the 2016 recounts caught Skyhorse's attention and launched this journey. But this book also reaches back to Vermont in the 1980s, when I was a reporter and met Bernie Sanders and became press secretary on the first campaign electing him to the House. Bill Stetson led me to many people in Bernie's campaign and in Democratic Party circles, including some who freely gave insights but asked not to be named, as they still work in politics.

The recounts put me back in touch with a community of activists, attorneys, and journalists I met after Ohio's 2004 election. They include Mark Crispin Miller, Bob Fitrakis, Jonathan Simon, Harvey

Wasserman, John Brakey, and others. Special thanks go to Don Hazen who has supported my work for many years at AlterNet starting with covering voting rights in 2008, and Bill Moyers and the Schumann Center for Media and Democracy.

I also must thank David Becker and John Lindback, who let me assist Pew's effort in 2010 to modernize voter registration and in so doing introduced me to many dedicated civil servants, academics, and technologists who want to improve elections and expand the vote. They gave me a greater appreciation of the complexity and layers involved in the process and still do.

Then there are the election law groups and affiliated scholars whose work has helped to document and quantify how voters are marginalized on partisan lines. These include the Brennan Center for Justice at New York University School of Law, Advancement Project, NAACP Legal Defense Fund, Demos and others cited in the endnotes. Their reports, legal briefs, and resulting court rulings from their work all contributed—as did legal documents, reports, and other records from those who wanted to tilt the field.

There are also many analysts and journalists who I have not met but whose work informs these pages. These include the Cook Political Report's David Wasserman, FiveThirtyEight's Harry Enten, and many excellent reporters at the *Washington Post*, *The New York Times*, Bloomberg, *Politico*, *USA Today*, *The Atlanta Journal-Constitution*, Reuters, *The Chicago Tribune*, The Intercept, Associated Press, and local TV.

Numerous books also contributed. Especially noteworthy are those by Michael Waldman and David Daley. David was very generous with his time and encouraged this effort to peel back the layers of how elections are structured. Other big contributions include drawing on voluminous reporting from *The Nation*'s Ari Berman, efforts pressing public officials for answers by Greg Palast, and videos by filmmaker Lulu Friesdat. Pro-democracy activists also played a part, such as early postelection analyses by Election Justice USA, recount organizers like Warren Linney, and Verified Voting's Barbara Simon. Thanks to Keith Conkin for proofreading drafts and suggesting what needed clarification.

I must also thank my family for their support and encouragement. My parents, Ronnie and Sheldon Rosenfeld, continue to encourage me and take pride in my work; my siblings for their feedback; Beth and Danya Sauerhaft who marveled that I made and met my deadlines.

But most of all, I want to thank my partner, Lynda Beth Unkeless, who encouraged this project from the start, was endlessly patient as it took up our spare time, and still found surprises and contributions in libraries and articles that sharpened its content and focus.

Finally, I thank my editor, Jonathan McCullough, for his incisive eye and comments taking the manuscript to a higher level.

ENDNOTES

Introduction

1. "It's time to bust the myth: Most Trump voters were not working class," by Nicholas Carnes and Noam Lupu, *Washington Post*, June 5, 2017. This report said two-thirds of Trump's voters earned more than the annual national median household income. https://www.washingtonpost.com/news/monkey-cage/wp/2017/06/05/its-time-to-bust-the-myth-most-trump-voters-were-not-working-class/?utm_term=.fc6044e39471&tid=a_inl.

2. "New Video: Watch Wisconsin Election Officials Reject Hand Counts After Electronic Scanners Make Big Mistake: 'I am just stunned at how inaccurate the whole thing is,'" by Lulu Friesdat, AlterNet.org, December 16, 2016, http://www.alternet.org/new-video-watch-wisconsin-election-officials-reject-hand-counts-after-electronic-scanners-make-big.

3. "Trump Is Dividing The Country, US Voters Say 2–1, Quinnipiac University National Poll Finds; Most Trust Media More Than President," Quinnipiac University, August 23, 2017, https://poll.qu.edu/national/release-detail?ReleaseID=2482.
    Also see: "Fox News Poll: Voters' mood sours, 56 percent say Trump tearing country apart," by Dana Blanton, FoxNews.com, August 30, 2017, "The number of voters happy with how things are going in the country is down 10 percentage points since April and stands at just 35 percent." http://www.foxnews.com/politics/2017/08/30/fox-news-poll-voters-mood-sours-56-percent-say-trump-tearing-country-apart.html.

SECTION I: THE DEMOCRATS
CHAPTER 1: BERNIE SANDERS

4.   "Democratic National Convention, 2016," *BallotPedia.org*. Sanders
      had 1,832 pledged delegates from the caucuses and primaries, 45
      percent, compared to Clinton's 2,219 pledged delegates. There
      were 713 superdelegates in addition. https://ballotpedia.org/
      Democratic_National_Convention,_2016.

5.   "Bernie 2016," Presidential Principle Campaign Committee, US Federal
      Election Commission. This is the FEC summary page, showing Sanders's
      campaign raised $237.6 million. https://www.fec.gov/data/committee/
      C00577130/?cycle=2016.

6.   "Revised Debate Memo," April 27, 2015, wikileaks.org. This email con-
      tains the Clinton campaign memo describing how the DNC coordinated
      with her campaign to schedule the televised debates in late 2015 and
      early 2016. After getting the schedule it sought, her campaign pushed
      the DNC to add another debate before the New Hampshire primary.
      https://www.wikileaks.org/podesta-emails/emailid/5688#searchresult.
      Also: "Leaked Email Proves DNC Rigged Primary Debates," by Dan
      Wright, shadowproof.com, October 12, 2016, https://shadowproof.com
      /2016/10/12/leaked-email-shows-dnc-rigged-primary-debates/.

7.   "Sanders campaign sues DNC after database breach," by Catherine
      Treyz, Dan Merica, Jeremy Diamond, Jeff Zeleny, CNN.com, December
      21, 2015, http://www.cnn.com/2015/12/18/politics/bernie-sanders-cam-
      paign-dnc-suspension/index.html.
      Also: "Debbie Wasserman Schultz: Give the voter file back to Bernie
      Sanders' campaign," Petition by Carl Gibson, *MoveOn.org*, https://pac.
      petitions.moveon.org/sign/debbie-wasserman-schultz-2.

CHAPTER 2: WHO WON IOWA?

8.   "The Iowa caucuses: An accident of history," by David Jackson,
      USA Today, January 29, 2016, http://www.desmoinesregister.com/story

/news/politics/elections/2016/01/29/iowa-caucuses-history-jimmy-carter-julian-zelizer/79426692/.

9. "Hunt Commission," wikipedia.org. The DNC convened the Hunt Commission in 1981 after a tumultuous 1980 convention, which, in turn, created its super-delegate system. https://en.wikipedia.org/wiki/Hunt_Commission.

10. Eugene V. Debs, wikipedia.org. Excerpt: "Debs ran as a Socialist candidate for President of the United States five times, including 1900 (earning 0.63% of the popular vote), 1904 (2.98%), 1908 (2.83%), 1912 (5.99%), and 1920 (3.41%), the last time from a prison cell." https://en.wikipedia.org/wiki/Eugene_V._Debs.

11. *Our Revolution: A Future to Believe In*, by Bernie Sanders, Thomas Dunne Books, 2016. p. 170–171. https://us.macmillan.com/ourrevolution/berniesanders/9781250132925.

12. "Editorial: Something smells in the Democratic Party," *The Des Moines Register* editorial, February 3, 2016, questioning whether Clinton had won and noting the ineptly run contest. http://www.desmoinesregister.com/story/opinion/editorials/caucus/2016/02/03/editorial-something-smells-democratic-party/79777580/.

13. *Shattered: Inside Hillary Clinton's Doomed Campaign*, by Jonathan Allen and Amie Parnes, Crown, 2016, page 111, http://www.penguinrandomhouse.com/search/shattered?q=shattered.

14. "Statement on Hillary Clinton's Victory in the Iowa Caucus," by Hillary for America's Iowa State Director Matt Paul, February 2, 2016, https://www.hillaryclinton.com/briefing/statements/2016/02/02/iowa-caucus-victory/.

15. *Iowa's nightmare revisited: Was correct winner called?* Report by Jennifer Jacobs, Feb. 2, 2016, questioning the accuracy of Iowa's Democratic Caucus count and winner, http://www.desmoinesregister.com/story/news/elections/presidential/caucus/2016/02/02/iowas-nightmare-revisited-correct-winner-called-caucus-night/79702010/.

16. Same as 12: "Editorial: Something smells in the Democratic Party," *The Des Moines Register* editorial, February 3, 2016.

17. Same as 11: *Our Revolution: A Future to Believe In*, by Bernie Sanders. p. 167.

18. "Texas Democratic primary and caucuses, 2008," wikipedia.org. This entry recounts how Clinton's 2008 presidential campaign filed

challenges of the Texas caucus results, seeking to nullify the votes of tens of thousands of attendees. https://en.wikipedia.org/wiki/ Texas_Democratic_primary_and_caucuses,_2008.

CHAPTER 3: LAS VEGAS RULES

19. "Harry Reid delivers for Hillary Clinton: Nevada's 'neutral' power players may have saved a campaign and changed history." by Jon Ralston, *USA Today*, February 20, 2016, http://www.usatoday.com/story/opinion/2016/02/20/hillary-clinton-wins-nevada-caucus-harry-reid-culinary-union-jon-ralston/80688750/.
20. "Results from the 2016 Nevada GOP caucuses," by Lily Mihalik, Anthony Pesce and Ben Walsh, *Los Angeles Times*, February 23, 2016. This map shows Sanders winning Nevada's northern counties, including Reno and Carson City. http://graphics.latimes.com/election-2016-nevada-results/.
21. "Update: Suspicious votes, long times at Dem caucus," by Mark Robison, *Reno Gazette-Journal*, Feb. 20, 2016. This report categorizes more than a dozen problems associated with inexperience and mismanagement in running the Democratic caucuses in Reno. http://www.rgj.com/story/news/politics/2016/02/20/long-lines-too-few-ballots-dem-caucus-locations/80666630/.
22. "Don't Call It a Bern-Back: According to social media rumors, Bernie Sanders claimed a win in Nevada in a surprise post-caucus upset, but the reality was far more complex and less definitive," by Kim LaCapria, snopes.com, April 9, 2016. This report describes the next stage in Nevada's delegate selection process, county conventions, and statements by the campaigns about who was winning. http://www.snopes.com/bernie-sanders-won-nevada/.

CHAPTER 4: NEW QUESTIONS, NEW BARRIERS

23. "Democracy Lost: A Report on the Fatally Flawed 2016 Democratic Primaries," by *Election Justice USA*, August 2016, ElectionJusticeUSA.org.

See pages 36–48, for media exit poll discrepancies with official results. https://drive.google.com/file/d/0B5O9I4XJdSISNzJyaWIxaWpZWnM/view.

24. "There Were 5-Hour Lines to Vote in Arizona Because the Supreme Court Gutted the Voting Rights Act," by Ari Berman, *The Nation*, March 23, 2016, https://www.thenation.com/article/there-were-five-hour-lines-to-vote-in-arizona-because-the-supreme-court-gutted-the-voting-rights-act/.

    Also see: Democracy Diminished: State and Local Threats to Voting Post-Shelby County, Alabama v. Holder, by NAACP Legal Defense Fund, 2016, pages 9–12. These reports describe how hours-long delays in Maricopa County, due to switching from precinct voting to voting centers, had not been approved by the Justice Department before the US Supreme Court invalidated DOJ oversight in its 2013 ruling on the Voting Rights Act. http://www.naacpldf.org/files/publications/Democracy%20Diminished-State%20and%20Local%20Voting%20Changes%20Post-Shelby%20v.%20Holder_4.pdf.

25. Same as 23: See pages 13–17. "Democracy Lost: A Report on the Fatally Flawed 2016 Democratic Primaries," by *Election Justice USA*, August 2016.

26. Same as 11: *Our Revolution: A Future to Believe In,* by Bernie Sanders. p. 174.

27. "Closed primary," ballotpedia.org. This lists all states with closed presidential primaries. https://ballotpedia.org/Closed_primary.

28. "It's Far Harder To Change Parties In New York Than In Any Other State," by Leah Lebresco, FiveThirtyEight.com, April 19, 2016, https://fivethirtyeight.com/features/its-far-harder-to-change-parties-in-new-york-than-in-any-other-state/.

29. Same as 11: *Our Revolution: A Future to Believe In,* by Bernie Sanders. p. 175.

30. *Justice Department Suing NYC Board Of Elections Over Last Year's Pre-Primary Mass Voter Purge*, by Nathan Tempey, gothamist.com, January 13, 2017. This report recounts the sloppy voter purge by Kings County (Brooklyn) before the 2016 Democratic presidential primary that led to 122,000 infrequent voters being removed. http://gothamist.com/2017/01/13/doj_sues_boe_brooklyn_voter_rolls.php.

31. Same as 30: *Justice Department Suing NYC Board Of Elections Over Last Year's Pre-Primary Mass Voter Purge*, by Nathan Tempey, gothamist.com.

32. "Statement From A. G. Schneiderman On Voting Issues During New York's Primary Election," The New York State Office of the Attorney General, April 20, 2016. "I am deeply troubled by the volume and consistency of voting irregularities, both in public reports and direct complaints to my office's voter hotline, which received more than one thousand complaints in the course of the day yesterday." https://ag.ny.gov/press-release/statement-ag-schneiderman-voting-issues-during-new-york%E2%80%99s-primary-election.

33. Same as 11: *Our Revolution: A Future to Believe In,* by Bernie Sanders. p. 178.

CHAPTER 5: THE NOT-SO-GOLDEN STATE

34. Same as 11: *Our Revolution: A Future to Believe In*, by Bernie Sanders. p. 179.

35. "Would-be independents joining the American Independent Party could blame California's voter registration card," by Jon Myers, *Los Angeles Times*, April 19, 2016. Excerpt: "A Times investigation found widespread confusion among California voters who choose the American Independent Party, an ultra-conservative organization that's been largely invisible from most campaigns. A poll of AIP voters found 73% mistakenly thought they were 'independent' of all parties. Those voters should have chosen the 'no party preference' option." http://www.latimes.com/politics/la-pol-ca-american-independent-party-california-voter-registration-card-20160419-story.html.

36. "Primary Elections in California," by Alex Padilla, California Secretary of State.

     This page from the Secretary of State's website explains how the Democratic presidential primary allows independent voters to cast ballots in the party's contest. "The Democratic and American Independent parties notified the Secretary of State that they will allow voters who did not state a political party preference to vote the presidential ballot of their parties in the upcoming June 7, 2016, Presidential Primary Election. Their notifications can be found in CC/ROV Memorandum #16036 (PDF)." http://www.sos.ca.gov/elections/primary-elections-california/.

37. "Snagged Votes In Los Angeles," by Judy Frankel, *Huffington Post*, July 5,

2016. This report notes certain counties opted for special crossover ballots for independent, or nonparty preference (NNP), voters, and the confusion in Los Angeles over handling these ballots. http://www.huffingtonpost.com/judy-frankel/snagged-votes-in-los-angeles_b_10794718.html.

38. "AP count: Clinton has delegates to win Democratic nomination," by Hope Yen, Stephen Ohlemacher, Lisa Lerer and Catherine Lucey, The Associated Press, June 7, 2016. This report, dateline Los Angeles, announced the Democratic nomination was locked up by Clinton one day before California held its presidential primary. https://apnews.com/4c9c850385c84b12ad5b85fda49743f9/after-weekend-wins-clinton-cusp-democratic-nomination.

39. Same as 11: *Our Revolution: A Future to Believe In*, by Bernie Sanders. p. 179.

40. "California Democratic primary, 2016," wikipedia.org. This report of the final vote count shows Hillary Clinton's election night margin of 14 percent shrinking to 7 percent after all California primary ballots were counted. https://en.wikipedia.org/wiki/California_Democratic_primary,_2016.

Chapter 6: The Democratic National Committee

41. "DNC Chair Says Superdelegates Exist to Protect Party Leaders," by Independent Voter, YouTube.com, February 12, 2016. This video clip shows a Feb. 12, 2016, CNN interview where DNC Chairwoman Debbie Wasserman Schultz said that superdelegates ensure inclusivity but also ward against grassroots activists. https://www.youtube.com/watch?v=w5llLIKM9Yc.

42. "The 4 Most Damaging Emails From the DNC WikiLeaks Dump," by Alana Abrasion and Shushannah Walsh, *ABC News*, July 25, 2016, http://abcnews.go.com/Politics/damaging-emails-dnc-wikileaks-dump/story?id=40852448.

43. "Carol Wilding et al vs. DNC Services Corporation and Deborah Wasserman Schultz," United States District Court, Southern District of Florida, Case 0:16-cv-61511-XXXX, entered June 28, 2016. This class-action lawsuit, filed by Sanders supporters against the DNC before the Democratic Convention, accuses the party of violating its charter to be a neutral party in nominating contests and cites Wikileaks' email hacks as

evidence. http://jampac.us/wp-content/uploads/2016/06/1-CLASS-AC-TION-COMPLAINT-6-28-16.pdf.

44.   "Will Keith Ellison Move the Democrats Left? By running for the D.N.C. chair, the Minnesota congressman hopes to lead a populist opposition against Trump," by Vinson Cunningham, *The New Yorker*, February 27, 2017. This profile of a bid by Rep. Keith Ellison, D-MN, to be DNC chair gives two more examples of the DNC colluding with Clinton's campaign in the primary season. First is establishing a joint fund-raising operation before the national party convention. Second is ex-chairwoman Donna Brazile, then a CNN commentator, alerting the campaign to questions for an upcoming televised debate. http://www.newyorker.com/magazine/2017/02/27/will-keith-ellison-move-the-democrats-left. Also see: "Donna Brazile," wikipedia.org. Brazile's biograhy, including stints as Al Gore's presidential campaign manager in 2000 and interim DNC chair in 2011. https://en.wikipedia.org/wiki/Donna_Brazile.

45.   "Top Democrat backpedals after saying primaries were 'rigged,'" by Yaron Steinbuch, *The New York Post*, Feb. 10. 2017. This report notes Tom Perez, then a candidate for DNC chair, told Kansas lawmakers that the 2016 nominating contest was rigged against Sanders, and then backtracked. http://nypost.com/2017/02/10/ex-labor-secretary-backpedals-on-rigged-democratic-primaries/.

46.   Same as 11: *Our Revolution: A Future to Believe In*, by Bernie Sanders. p. 195.

47.   Same as 11: *Our Revolution: A Future to Believe In*, by Bernie Sanders. p. 185, 197.

SECTION II: THE REPUBLICANS
Chapter 7. Gaming The Rules of Politics

48. "Why Did the Founding Fathers Choose a Republic?" by Thomas DeMichele, May 12, 2016, *FactMyth.com*. This article concisely describes why the United States is a republic with democratic features, but not a democracy where popular votes determine governing institutions. http://factmyth.com/why-did-the-founding-fathers-choose-a-republic/. Also see: "Child of the Enlightenment," by Garry Wills, *The New York Times* Magazine supplement, July 2, 2017. This describes the founder's competing considerations, including the distrust of popular factions and the belief the high reaches of government should be run by people of "sufficient virtue and intelligence." https://usedbooksinclass.com/tag/garry-wills-child-of-enlightenment/.

49. *The American Slave Coast: A History of the Slave-Breeding Industry*, by Ned and Constance Sublette, Lawrence Hill Books, 2016. This authoritative economic history of the Atlantic slave trade describes its impact on the colonial and pre-Civil War eras. http://www.chicagoreviewpress.com/american-slave-coast—the-products-9781613748206.php.

50. *The Great Suppression: Voting Rights, Corporate Cash, and the Conservative Assault on Democracy*, by Zachary Roth, Crown, 2016. See Introduction and Chapter 4. Also same as 47: Garry Wills' *New York Times* Magazine special section.

51. "ALEC Is Talking About Changing the Way Senators Are Elected and Taking Away Your Vote: A proposed resolution advocates for overturning the 17th Amendment so Republican-controlled state legislatures could pick senators," by John Nichols, *The Nation*, July 18, 2017, https://www.thenation.com/article/alec-wants-to-to-change-the-way-senators-are-elected-and-take-away-your-vote/.

52. *The Fight to Vote*, by Michael Waldman, Simon and Schuster, 2016, http://www.simonandschuster.com/books/The-Fight-to-Vote/Michael-Waldman/9781501116483.

53. "United States House of Representatives elections, 2012," wikipedia.org. Excerpt: "Although Democratic candidates received a nationwide plurality of more than 1.4 million votes (1.2%) in all House elections, the

Republican Party won a 33-seat advantage in the state-apportioned totals, thus retaining its House majority by 17 seats." https://en.wikipedia.org/wiki/United_States_House_of_Representatives_elections,_2012.

54. "United States House of Representatives elections, 2016," wikipedia.org, https://en.wikipedia.org/wiki/United_States_House_of_Representatives_elections,_2016.

55. *2016 Pre- and Post-Election State Legislative Control*, by National Conference of State Legislatures, November 9, 2016. Excerpt: "This map shows post-election legislative control as of Wednesday morning. Republicans control both chambers of the legislature in 32 states, Democrats control both chambers of the legislature in 13 states and three states split control." http://www.ncsl.org/research/elections-and-campaigns/2016-pre-and-post-election-state-legislative-control.aspx.

56. "October House Overview: GOP Risk Factors," by David Wasserman, *The Cook Political Report*, October 17, 2013. Redistricting expert Wasserman writes the GOP has a 6.8 percent head start in the competitive congressional races that will determine the House majority in 2014's elections. "By our calculations, House Democrats would need to win the national popular vote for the House by between six and seven points in order to win the barest possible majority of 218 seats. How did we calculate this? In 2012, Democratic candidates won 49.16 percent of the national popular House vote to 48.03 for Republicans, but only won 201 of 435 seats. If every seat shifted uniformly in Democrats' direction, Democrats' lead nationally would have needed to expand to roughly 6.8 percent to drag 17 more GOP-won seats to Democrats' side." http://cookpolitical.com/story/6330.

Also see: "A Very Early Look At The Battle For The House In 2018: Donald Trump is unpopular enough that Republicans could lose the House, but there's a lot of uncertainty." by Harry Enten, FiveThirtyEight.com, February 15, 2017. Enten writes the GOP has a 5.5 to 8.0 percent starting line advantage due to 2011's extreme redistricting in the races that will control the House in 2018's election. "Democrats are essentially spotting the GOP 5.5 points in the battle for control of the House. And even that may be underestimating Republicans ability to win a majority of seats without a majority of the vote. Since 2012 (or when most states instituted the current House district lines),

Republicans have won, on average, 51 percent of the two-party House vote and 55 percent of House seats. If that difference holds for 2018, Democrats would need to win the House popular vote by about 8 percentage points to win half the House seats." https://fivethirtyeight.com/features/a-very-early-look-at-the-battle-for-the-house-in-2018/.

57.   *Ratf**ked: The True Story Behind the Secret Plan to Steal America's Democracy*, by David Daley, Norton, 2016, http://books.wwnorton.com/books/Ratfked/.

58.   "The GOP Targets State Legislatures: He who controls redistricting can control Congress," by Karl Rove, *The Wall Street Journal*, March 4, 2010. Rove's commentary laying out the RedMap plan began, "The political world is fixated on whether this year's elections will deliver an epic rebuke of President Barack Obama and his party. If that happens, it could end up costing Democrats congressional seats for a decade to come." https://www.wsj.com/articles/SB100014240527487038627045750996706889398044.

59.   "2011 State and Legislative Partisan Composition," National Conference of State Legislatures. For 2011, when stage legislatures or commissions redrew legislative and US House districts, Democrats fully controlled eleven states: AR, CA, CN, DE, HI, IL, MD, MA, VT, VA, and WV. Republicans controlled twenty states: AL, AZ, FL, GA, ID, IN, KS, ME, MI, ND, OH, OK, PA, SC, SD, TN, TX, UT, WS, and WY. http://www.ncsl.org/documents/statevote/LegisControl_2011.pdf.

60.   "Supreme Court forced to confront the 'unsavory' politics of district lines," by Richard Wolf, *USA Today*, May 25, 2017. Wolf notes the blue states where extreme redistricting is most prevalent are MD, MA, IL. "In 2012, Republicans won 53% of the vote but 72% of the House seats in states where they drew the lines. Democrats won 56% of the vote but 71% of the seats where they controlled the process." https://www.usatoday.com/story/news/politics/2017/05/25/supreme-court-faces-decision-politics-election-districts/102020210/.
Also see: "The State of Redistricting Litigation (March 2017 edition)," Brennan Center for Justice at New York University Law School, https://www.brennancenter.org/blog/state-redistricting-litigation-march-2017-edition.

61. *Issues Related to State Voter Identification Laws*, US Government Accountability Office, September 2014. This report analyzes how stricter voter ID laws diminished turnout in Kansas and Tennessee. "GAO found that turnout among eligible and registered voters declined more in Kansas and Tennessee than it declined in comparison states—by an estimated 1.9 to 2.2 percentage points more in Kansas and 2.2 to 3.2 percentage points more in Tennessee—and the results were consistent across the different data sources and voter populations used in the analysis." https://www.gao.gov/products/GAO-14-634.

62. *Issues Related to Registering Voters and Administering Elections*, US Government Accountability Office, June 2016. This report has a chart on page 40 that shows same-day registration and voting by mail have the largest measurable effects of increasing turnout. http://www.gao.gov/assets/680/678131.pdf.

63. Baker v. Carr, Wikipedia. This is the US Supreme Court's 1962 decision stating the goal of redistricting was to create political districts based on the principle of one-person, one-vote. https://en.wikipedia.org/wiki/Baker_v._Carr.

64. Vieth v. Jubelirer [02–1580], FindLaw.com. The Supreme Court's 2004 ruling, *Vieth v. Jubelirer* where Justice Anthony Kennedy wrote said political "decorum" should guide mapmakers. http://caselaw.findlaw.com/us-supreme-court/541/267.html.

65. Same as 57: *Ratf**ked: The True Story Behind the Secret Plan to Steal America's Democracy*, by David Daley, Norton, 2016.

66. Same as 60: "The State of Redistricting Litigation (March 2017 edition)." This Brennan Center summary tracks federal redistricting litigation. The only challenge filed by Republicans against Democrats is in Maryland. It notes that redistricting cases fall under two categories, those challenging the illegal use of race and those asserting excessive partisanship.
Also see: "Republican redistricting is taking a beating in the courts, right now," by Amber Phillips, *The Washington Post*, January 28, 2017. This report summarizes recent rulings in federal court that have gone against the GOP. In Wisconsin, a district court found partisan advantage. In Texas, Alabama, Virginia, and North Carolina, the courts found

racial discrimination. https://www.washingtonpost.com/news/the-fix/ wp/2017/01/28/republican-redistricting-is-taking-a-beating-in-the-courts-right-now/?utm_term=.0b9cfe552d74.

67. "Three Tests for Practical Evaluation of Partisan Gerrymandering," by Samuel S.-H. Wang, *Stanford Law Review*, June 2016. Princeton professor Samuel S. H. Wang's study concluding that gerrymanders had cost Democrats as many as twenty-two House seats in the 2012 election—nearly enough to flip the chamber's control. http://www.stanfordlawreview.org/ wp-content/uploads/sites/3/2016/06/3_-_Wang_-_Stan._L._Rev.pdf.

68. "New Report: Extreme Partisan Maps Account for 16–17 Republican Seats in Congress," Brennan Center for Justice, May 16, 2017. This study finds sixteen to seventeen GOP House seats are affected by extreme redistricting. https://www.brennancenter.org/press-release/new-report-extreme-partisan-maps-account-16-17-republican-seats-congress.

69. Same as 55. NCSL report. *2016 Pre- and Post-Election State Legislative Control*, by National Conference of State Legislatures, November 9, 2016.

70. Same as 56: "A Very Early Look At The Battle For The House In 2018: Donald Trump is unpopular enough that Republicans could lose the House, but there's a lot of uncertainty," by Harry Enten, FiveThirtyEight. com, February 15, 2017.

71. Same as 66: "The State of Redistricting Litigation (March 2017 edition)," by the Brennan Center For Justice, and "Republican redistricting is taking a beating in the courts, right now," by Amber Phillips, *The Washington Post*, January 28, 2017.

72. See 59 for GOP-held states in 2011. Also: "When Does Political Gerrymandering Cross a Constitutional Line?" by Adam Liptak, *The New York Times*, May 15, 2017. This update on gerrymandering says the Supreme Court has never struck down a map based on outsized partisan gains, and describes the analysis that is being used in the Wisconsin partisan-based challenge that calculates what are called wasted votes. It lists the states with biggest "wasted vote" gaps. Republican-held: FL, IN, KS, MI, MO, NC, OH, VA, WS, WY; Democrat-held: NY, RI. https://www .nytimes.com/2017/05/15/us/politics/when-does-political-gerrymandering-cross-a-constitutional-line.html?rref=collection%2Fbyline%2Fadam-lipta k&action=click&contentCollection=undefined&region=stream&module=s tream_unit&version=latest&contentPlacement=3&pgtype=collection.

73. Same as 56: "A Very Early Look At The Battle For The House In 2018: Donald Trump is unpopular enough that Republicans could lose the House, but there's a lot of uncertainty." by Harry Enten, FiveThirtyEight.com, February 15, 2017.

74. "Republican redistricting is taking a beating in the courts (again)," by Amber Phillips, *The Washington Post*, May 22, 2017. This article reviews recent federal court redistricting decisions (NC, VA, TX, AL, WS) and notes that they stemmed from Republicans winning twenty-one state chambers in 2010. It also notes that the November 2016 ruling against Wisconsin's GOP was the first federal court ruling in a decade that voided a map on excessive partisan grounds. The Supreme Court will hear an appeal in its fall 2017 term. https://www.washingtonpost.com/news/the-fix/wp/2017/05/22/republican-redistricting-is-taking-a-beating-in-the-courts-again/?utm_term=.499e563318b8.

75. "Key Question for Supreme Court: Will It Let Gerrymanders Stand?" by Michael Wines, *The New York Times*, April 21, 2017. This article previews the Wisconsin gerrymandering case that's headed to the Supreme Court in the fall 2018 term. It notes how a lower federal court agreed with Democrats that it was an unconstitutional partisan power grab, but also that the US Supreme Court has never thrown out maps on partisan greed. (It doesn't discuss the other gerrymandering cases that are illegal, which is why they are based on overt and provable racial discrimination.) It also references the Court's 2004 ruling, in *Vieth v. Jubelirer*, where Justice Kennedy wrote said political "decorum" should guide mapmakers. https://www.nytimes.com/2017/04/21/us/democrats-gerrymander-supreme-court.html?ref=todayspaper&_r=0.

76. Same as 60: "The State of Redistricting Litigation (March 2017 edition)," by the Brennan Center For Justice.

77. Cooper v. Harris, The US Supreme Court's May 2017 ruling 5 to 3 that North Carolina's 2011 gerrymander of two US House districts was racially discriminatory and unconstitutional. The dissent, starting on page 46, by Justice Samuel Alito and agreed to by Chief Justice John Roberts and Associate Justice Anthony Kennedy said the majority went looking for race, adding that extreme partisan redistricting was constitutional. https://www.supremecourt.gov/opinions/16pdf/15-1262_db8e.pdf.

78. "For Voting Rights Advocates, Court Decision Is 'Temporary Victory,'"

by Michael Wines, *The New York Times*, May 16, 2017. This analysis, coming after the Supreme Court's North Carolina ruling that concluded that the state's 2011 gerrymander was racially discriminatory, suggested that ruling was a temporary victory in a longer war. It discussed how the Court sees the two categories of gerrymandering cases, extreme partisanship and racial discrimination, differently, even as it struggles to separate them when those factors overlap. https://www.nytimes.com/2017/05/16/us/for-voting-rights-advocates-court-decision-is-temporary-victory.html?_r=0.

Also see tweets by nationally known redistricting expert, University of Florida's Michael McDonald, who notes the North Carolina dissent by conservatives doesn't bode well for Wisconsin Democrat's excessive partisanship argument: https://twitter.com/ElectProject/status/866675389778624512.

79. Same as 75: "Key Question for Supreme Court: Will It Let Gerrymanders Stand?" by Michael Wines, *The New York Times*, April 21, 2017. Also see 77, Cooper v. Harris, with dissent by Justice Samuel Alito starting on page 46.

80. "Revised Redistricting Plans Face Strong Public Opposition: GOP lawmakers on a key Senate committee approved a revision Friday of controversial redistricting plans, but Democrats and others accused Republicans of lacking transparency," by Ezra Kaplan, Associated Press, March 24, 2017. This report about revising Georgia's state legislative districts had Democrats accusing majority Republicans of steamrolling the process by acting secretly and still maintaining an advantage. "Jerry Gonzalez, the CEO of the Georgia Association of Latino Elected Officials, is concerned that the lack of transparency could have more nefarious results. 'Elected officials are rigging the system to racially pick their voters,' Gonzalez said to the committee. 'This process occurred under the cover of darkness and without public input.'" https://www.usnews.com/news/best-states/georgia/articles/2017-03-24/revised-redistricting-plans-face-strong-public-opposition.

81. "Senate Approves Redistricting Plan; Black Democrats Object: The Alabama Senate approved new legislative districts over the objections of black Democrats," by Kim Chandler, The Associated Press, May 4, 2017. This report says the GOP's redrawn state legislative districts in Alabama still are not fair. "A contentious point in the debate was control of Jefferson

County, home to the state's largest city, Birmingham, which is majority black and often the focus of partisan disputes over legislation impacting local governments. Democrats want an even number of Democrats and Republicans in the Jefferson County delegation. The Republican map, however, creates districts that would most likely elect four Republicans and three Democrats. The current split is five Republicans and three Democrats. Sen. Rodger Smitherman, D-Birmingham, said the GOP-drawn map stretches suburban districts into the county to maintain GOP control. 'It has smidgens of Jim Crow,' Smitherman said." https://www.usnews.com/news/best-states/alabama/articles/2017-05-04/senate-approves-redistricting-plan.

82. "With Supreme Court appeal, Texas wants to keep congressional map intact: Attorney General Ken Paxton revealed that Texas has no plans to ask lawmakers to redraw the state's Congressional map in a fresh round of legislative overtime. Instead, Paxton is appealing the ruling to the US Supreme Court," by Jim Malewitz, *The Texas Tribune*, August 18, 2017, https://www.texastribune.org/2017/08/18/paxton-redistricting-filing/.

83. "A Harsh Dose of Electoral Reality: Democrats Have Uphill Battle in '18 and Need to Elect Governors to Fight Gerrymandered GOP Monopoly," by Steven Rosenfeld, AlterNet.org, April 7, 2017. Excerpt: "'There is no question that Republican-led gerrymandering in 2011 has rigged the system against Democrats . . . What we need to do is level the playing field, unrig that system, so that Democrats can compete and we can translate those campaign tactics into electoral success that actually reflects the will of the voters, which is not happening right now,' Kelly Ward, executive director of the newly formed National Democratic Redistricting Committee said. 'That is what the National Democratic Redistricting Committee is trying to lead.'" http://www.alternet.org/activism/democratic-partys-future-hinges-more-winning-2018-governors-races-taking-back-house.

84. "The Supreme Court Could Make It Easier for States to Purge Voters; The Court has decided to hear a new case from Ohio, where Democrats were twice as likely as Republicans to be purged from the rolls in the state's largest counties." by Ari Berman, *TheNation.com*, May 30, 2017. This article reports on Ohio's voter purges of infrequent voters that are at the center of a case to be heard by the Supreme Court in its fall 2017 term.

"From 2011 to 2016, Ohio purged 2 million voters from the rolls—1.2 million for infrequent voting—more than any other state." https://www.thenation.com/article/supreme-court-make-easier-states-purge-voters/.

85. *Judges Find Wisconsin Redistricting Unfairly Favored Republicans*, by Michael Wines, November 21, 2017. This report discusses why the WI case is the first one in three decades to bring the issue of an unconstitutional partisan gerrymander to the Supreme Court. (It doesn't say that lower federal courts have been making these rulings.) It also notes that WI's partisan tilting of the playing field is of the same magnitude as VA, NC, and MI. https://www.nytimes.com/2016/11/21/us/wisconsin-redistricting-found-to-unfairly-favor-republicans.html?mcubz=2&_r=0.

Also see 72: "When Does Political Gerrymandering Cross a Constitutional Line?" by Adam Liptak, *The New York Times*, May 15, 2017. This analysis discusses why the WI case, even with its new math showing outsize partisan impacts benefiting GOP, faces an uphill fight at the Supreme Court. "The Supreme Court has never struck down an election map on the ground that it was drawn to make sure one political party would win an outsize number of seats. But it has left open the possibility that some kinds of political gamesmanship in redistricting may be too extreme."

Chapter 9. Looking Forward, Not Backward

86. *Deliver The Vote: A History of Election Fraud, An American Political Tradition—1742–2004*, by Tracy Campbell, Carroll & Graf Publishers, 2005. https://www.amazon.com/Deliver-Vote-Election-Political-Tradition-1742-2004/dp/078671591X.

87. Same as 52: *The Fight to Vote*, by Michael Waldman. For voter fraud investigation statistics, see pages 186, 187. For GAO study on impact of stricter voter ID requirements, see page 209. For Texas Republican Royal Masset's estimate of 3 percent reduction in Democratic turnout but to stricter voter ID laws, see page 190.

88. "Over 220,000 Ballots Didn't Count In The Presidential Primaries; Try to cast a regular ballot, rather than a provisional one, when voting this fall," by Samantha Lachman, *Huffington Post*, June 16, 2016, "Over 220,000 provisional ballots have already been discounted in the presi

dential primaries this year, according to a survey by *The Huffington Post*,
with many thousands more likely to be tossed as states finish certifying
their primaries." http://www.huffingtonpost.com/entry/provisional-ballots-
not-counted_us_5761bb92e4b0df4d586f15fe.

89. Same as 61: *Issues Related to State Voter Identification Laws*, US Government
Accountability Office, September 2014. This report discusses the most
authoritative research on voter fraud, says its occurrence is exceptionally
rare—single-digit instances in state where million vote—and that no federal agency tracks it. That absence helps to perpetuate fictitious claims
about its presence. See numbered pages 62–74. "Based on our own review
of federal and state information sources, we identified challenges such as
there is no single source of information on possible instances of in-person voter fraud and variation exists among federal and state sources in
the extent to which they collect information on election fraud."

90. "New Voting Restrictions in America," by the Brennan Center for Justice,
2016. This is an interactive webpage and map that details restrictive voting laws passed by states since the 2011 gerrymander. Of the twenty states
listed, only two—Rhode Island and Illinois—are reliably blue. "Overall,
20 states have new restrictions in effect since then—10 states have more
restrictive voter ID laws in place (and six states have strict photo ID
requirements), seven have laws making it harder for citizens to register,
six cut back on early voting days and hours, and three made it harder to
restore voting rights for people with past criminal convictions." https://
www.brennancenter.org/new-voting-restrictions-america.

91. "Debunking the Voter Fraud Myth," by the Brennan Center for Justice,
January 31, 2017. This is the center's most up-to-date report on this issue.
It found most purported incidents of voter fraud are traceable to other
causes, such as clerical errors or bad data matching. The report reviewed
elections that had been meticulously studied for voter fraud, and found
incident rates between 0.0003 percent and 0.0025 percent. It is more
likely that an American "will be struck by lightning than that he will
impersonate another voter at the polls." https://www.brennancenter.org/
analysis/debunking-voter-fraud-myth.

92. Texas NAACP v. Steen (consolidated with Veasey v. Abbott), the
Brennan Center for Justice, July 6, 2017. This webpage gives the history of the cases, *NAACP v. Steen*: https://www.brennancenter.org/

legal-work/naacp-v-steen This is the US District Court ruling issued on April 10, 2017, https://www.brennancenter.org/sites/default/files/legal-work/2017-04-10_Order_Intent.pdf.

93. *The Deceit of Voter Fraud*, by Bob Hall and Isela Gutierrez, Democracy North Carolina, April 2017. This report details how Gov. Pat McCrory's reelection campaign fabricated voter fraud charges against six hundred people in a failed attempt to overturn the results of his narrow loss in November 2016. It includes the sloppy analysis used, interviews with victims, and even comments by Republican activists who dutifully filed charges contesting these voters registrations but who were left empty-handed by McCrory's campaign during subsequent hearings by county boards of election. http://nc-democracy.org/wp-content/uploads/2017/04/FraudReport.pdf.

94. *A Sampling of Election Fraud Cases From Across The Country*, The Heritage Foundation, 2017. This report lists 492 cases and 733 convictions of false voter registrations, noncitizen voting, fraudulent use of absentee ballots, and duplicate voting from 1984 through 2017. http://thf-legal.s3.amazonaws.com/VoterFraudCases.pdf.

95. "Voter Turnout in Presidential Elections: 1828–2012," The American Presidency Project, University of California Santa Barbara. This chart lists the presidential election turnout through 2012. http://www.presidency.ucsb.edu/data/turnout.php. Also see, "2016 November General Election Turnout Rates," The United States Election Project, the University of Florida. This chart lists the 2016 turnout. Together, 980 million people voted for president between 1984 and 2016. http://www.electproject.org/2016g.

96. "Voting Laws Roundup 2017," by the Brennan Center for Justice, May 10, 2017. Excerpt: "At this point in the year, every state's legislature is either in session or has completed its 2017 calendar. As has been the case all decade, legislators across the country are trying to reshape state voting laws. In several places, this means it will soon be harder to vote: Five states have already enacted bills to cut back on voting access, and one more is on the verge of doing so. By comparison, three states enacted voting restrictions in 2015 and 2016 combined." https://www.brennancenter.org/analysis/voting-laws-roundup-2017.

97. "Hearing Before The Committee on House Administration, Columbus Ohio, March 21, 2005." This is the transcript and submissions, including

testimony by Mark "Thor" Hearne. https://babel.hathitrust.org/cgi/pt?i
d=pur1.32754078873928;view=1up;seq=31.

98. Same as 97: All the quotations in the paragraphs that follow are from this
source.

99. Same as 97: Hearne testimony and submitted report begin on page 273.

100. Same as 97.

101. *What Happened in Ohio? A Documentary Record of Theft and Fraud in the 2004
Election*, by Robert J. Fitrakis, Steven Rosenfeld and Harvey Wasserman,
The New Press, 2006. Pages 306–313 summarize impact of anti-voter
actions taken by Secretary of State Kenneth Blackwell. http://thenew-
press.com/books/what-happened-ohio.

102. Same as 52: *The Fight to Vote*, by Michael Waldman. See pages 186–7
for examples of voter fraud that federal investigations found—all were
errors or small-time ploys unworthy of Justice Department scrutiny.
http://www.simonandschuster.com/books/The-Fight-to-Vote/
Michael-Waldman/9781501116483.

103. "Why Republicans Can't Find the Big Voter Fraud Conspiracy: If the
last federal investigation is any guide, the answer is simple: It probably
doesn't exist," by Lisa Rab, *Politico Magazine*, April 2, 2017. This feature
reviews the history of the GOP's pursuit of voter fraud, including the
George W. Bush administration's firing on federal prosecutors for failing to deliver voter fraud convictions, the DOJ's investigation results
and prosecutions, and other evidence pointing to its real-life status as
a political fiction. http://www.politico.com/magazine/story/2017/04/
why-republicans-cant-find-the-big-voter-fraud-conspiracy-214972.

104. "ACORN Accusations: McCain makes exaggerated claims of 'voter
fraud.' Obama soft-pedals his connections," by Jess Henig, October 21,
2008, http://www.factcheck.org/2008/10/acorn-accusations/.

105. "Election 2012: Voting Laws Roundup," by the Brennan Center for
Justice, October 11, 2012, http://www.brennancenter.org/analysis/election-
2012-voting-laws-roundup.

CHAPTER 10: THE VOTING WARS

106. Same as 52: *The Fight to Vote*, by Michael Waldman. See page 186–7
for federal voter fraud investigations, page 190 for estimate by Texas

Republican Party's Royal Masset that stricter voter ID laws would undercut Democratic turnout by 3 percent, and page 209 for GAO studies. http://www.simonandschuster.com/books/The-Fight-to-Vote/ Michael-Waldman/9781501116483.

107. Same as 61: *Issues Related to State Voter Identification Laws*, US Government Accountability Office, September 2014.

108. "Voter Suppression Works," by Sean McElwee, demos.org, May 9, 2017. This study on the impact of stricter voter ID compared laws between red and blue states. It found stricter ID laws in Mississippi, Virginia, and Wisconsin caused turnout to drop by 1.7 percent. When Wisconsin was compared to Minnesota, turnout fell by 2.2 percent in high black population counties. http://www.demos.org/blog/5/9/17/ voter-suppression-works.

109. "Do voter identification laws suppress minority voting? Yes. We did the research." by Zoltan Hajnal, Nazita Lajevardi, Lindsay Nielson, *The Washington Post*, February 15, 2017. This analysis suggests that stricter voter ID laws undercut progressive candidates in primaries and pushes the Democratic Party toward the center. "All else equal, when strict ID laws are instituted, the turnout gap between Republicans and Democrats in primary contests more than doubles from 4.3 points to 9.8 points. Likewise, the turnout gap between conservative and liberal voters more than doubles from 7.7 to 20.4 points . . . Unsurprisingly, these strict ID laws are passed almost exclusively by Republican legislatures." https://www.washingtonpost.com/news/monkey-cage/wp/2017/02/15/ do-voter-identification-laws-suppress-minority-voting-yes-we-did-the-research/?utm_term=.a248da5d08ce.

110. "Voting Law Changes: Election Update," by Wendy Weiser and Diana Kasdan, The Brennan Center for Justice, October 28, 2012. http://www. brennancenter.org/publication/voting-law-changes-election-update.

111. "The Voting Rights Act of 1965," The US Department of Justice. This is the DOJ's online description of the history of the Voting Rights Act and subsequent amendments in 1970, 1975, 1982, and 2006. https://www.jus-tice.gov/crt/history-federal-voting-rights-laws.

112. Same as 110: "Voting Law Changes: Election Update," by Wendy Weiser and Diana Kasdan, The Brennan Center for Justice, October 28, 2012.

113. Shelby County v. Holder, The Supreme Court's 2013 *Shelby County v.*

Holder decision striking down the enforcement formula in Section 5 as unconstitutional, https://www.supremecourt.gov/opinions/12pdf/12-96 _6k47.pdf.

114. "About Section 5 of the Voting Rights Act," The US Department of Justice. This is the DOJ's summary of states and counties previously covered under Section 5 of the Voting Rights Act. https://www.justice.gov/crt/about-section-5-voting-rights-act.

115. "Special Report: Behind US race cases, a little-known recruiter," by Joan Biskupic, Reuters, December 4, 2012. Excerpt: "Over the past 20 years, Blum has similarly launched at least a dozen lawsuits attacking race-based protections. In addition to the Fisher [affirmative action in university admissions] and *Shelby County* [Voting Rights Act] cases, two other Blum-backed cases reached the Supreme Court. One struck down majority-black and majority-Latino voting districts in Texas. The other prompted the court to suggest it might eliminate a major portion of the Voting Rights Act of 1965, which the conservative-majority bench may now be poised to do." http://www.reuters.com/article/us-usa-court-casemaker-idUSBRE8B30V220121204.

Also see: "Meet the Brains Behind the Effort to Get the Supreme Court to Rethink Civil Rights: Edward Blum has orchestrated a string of big cases targeting voting rights and affirmative action," by Stephanie Mencimer, Mother Jones, March/April 2016. http://www.motherjones.com/politics/2016/04/edward-blum-supreme-court-affirmative-action-civil-rights.

116. "The GOP is Dying Off. Literally," by Daniel J. McGraw, May 17, 2015, *Politico Magazine*. http://www.politico.com/magazine/story/2015/05/the-gop-is-dying-off-literally-118035.

117. "Voting Law Roundup 2013," by the Brennan Center for Justice, Dec. 19, 2013. This summary lists the 2013 legislation and resulting laws that would restrict and also expand voting rights following the Supreme Court's *Shelby County* ruling. Typically, red states, including some presidential swing states, moved to restrict rights, while blue states went in the opposite direction. http://www.brennancenter.org/analysis/election-2013-voting-laws-roundup Also see: "Voting Laws Roundup 2014," by the Brennan Center for Justice, December 18, 2014. http://www.brennancenter.org/analysis/voting-laws-roundup-2014.

118. Same as 114. "About Section 5 of the Voting Rights Act," Department of Justice.

119. Same as 24: Democracy Diminished: State and Local Threats to Voting Post-Shelby County, Alabama v. Holder, by NAACP Legal Defense Fund, June 9, 2016. This report details post-*Shelby* voter suppression tactics and legal fights that continued into the 2016 election. It has sections on Alabama, Arizona, Arkansas, Florida, Georgia, North Carolina, South Carolina, and also describes the fight over requiring documented proof of citizenship on voter registration forms at US Election Assistance Commission.

120. Same as 96: "Voting Laws Roundup 2017," by the Brennan Center for Justice, May 10, 2017. This update notes that more anti-voter laws were passed in 2017 than in the two prior years, but notes that blue states have been looking at expanding voting rights. Those blue states are not considered swing states for the House majority or presidential elections.

121. "Supreme Court: Virginia redistricting must be reexamined for racial bias," by Robert Barnes, *Chicago Tribune*, March 1, 2017. This report discusses the Supreme Court's ruling that sent the Virginia redistricting case back to lower courts to assess the latest maps. While it is nominally a victory for minority voters and Democrats, the political boundaries that have been challenged as racially discriminatory remain. http://www.chicagotribune.com/news/nationworld/ct-supreme-court-virginia-redistricting-racial-bias-20170301-story.html.

Also see: "Will third time be a charm for those who want NC Supreme Court to invalidate election maps?" by Anne Blythe, *The News and Observer*, May 30, 2017. This report recounts how the North Carolina GOP has thwarted repeated federal court rulings to redraw state and congressional district maps. http://www.newsobserver.com/news/politics-government/politics-columns-blogs/under-the-dome/article153347589.html.

Also see: "Revised Redistricting Plans Face Strong Public Opposition: GOP lawmakers on a key Senate committee approved a revision Friday of controversial redistricting plans, but Democrats and others accused Republicans of lacking transparency," by Ezra Kaplan, Associated Press, March 24, 2017. This AP report about revising Georgia state legislative districts also had Democrats accusing the majority GOP of acting secretly to retain their advantage. https://

www.usnews.com/news/best-states/georgia/articles/2017-03-24/revised-redistricting-plans-face-strong-public-opposition.

122. "Alabama's GOP approves new maps; Dems vow repeat court fight: Alabama's overwhelmingly Republican legislature has sent a new legislative map to the governor after a rancorous session featuring a racially charged email comparing lawmakers to monkeys." by Kim Chandler, Associated Press, May 20, 2017. What's unfolded in Alabama is typical of GOP efforts to keep their structural advantage despite losing in court. "'It seems like we are going to end up in court again,' said Legislative Black Caucus Chairman John Knight, D-Montgomery. 'It's clear. You can look at the [newly redrawn] map. There is racial gerrymandering.'" https://www.apnews.com/526ad1f61e32407ab28c40616efbbcd7.

123. Same as 24: Democracy Diminished: State and Local Threats to Voting Post-Shelby County, Alabama v. Holder, by NAACP Legal Defense Fund, June 9, 2016.

124. "Plaintiffs Claim Bias During Closing Argument Against Texas Voter ID Law," by Manny Fernandez, *The New York Times*, Sept. 22, 2014. Excerpt: "Richard Dellheim, a lawyer for the Justice Department's Voting Section, said in his closing argument that more than 608,000 registered voters in Texas lack the types of ID required by the law and that the percentage of Hispanics and blacks without the necessary identification is substantially higher than the percentage of whites without that ID . . . Texas has issued only 279 election ID cards. A similar program in Georgia has issued 2,200 cards, Mr. Dellheim said." https://www.nytimes.com/2014/09/23/us/plaintiffs-assert-bias-during-closing-argument-against-texas-voter-id-law.html?mcubz=2.

125. Same as the first item in 121: "Supreme Court: Virginia redistricting must be reexamined for racial bias," by Robert Barnes, *Chicago Tribune*, March 1, 2017.

126. "Va. Supreme Court strikes down McAuliffe's order on felon voting rights," by Graham Moomaw, *Richmond Times-Dispatch*, July 23, 2016. This report recounts the state Supreme Court ruling that threw out Gov. McAuliffe's first executive order restoring ex-felon voting rights, which resulted in 11,662 ex-felons to register. Virginia's Supreme Court ordered those ex-felons to be removed from voter rolls. McAuliffe replied he'd take steps to reinstate their voting rights. http://www.richmond.com/news/

virginia/government-politics/va-supreme-court-strikes-down-mcauliffe-s-order-on-felon/article_718d04d8-70b2-5bfb-aa8c-0ff1ca108b8d.html.

127. "Governor McAuliffe Provides Update on Restoration of Rights Numbers," by WWIR, NBC29.com, January 18, 2018. This report describes McAuliffe's second clemency effort, which restored 140,000 ex-felon's voting rights. http://www.nbc29.com/story/34203534/governor-mcauliffe-provides-update-on-restoration-of-rights-numbers.

Also see: "Virginia's breakthrough on rectifying an enormous injustice," Editorial Board, *The Washington Post*, June 11, 2017. This editorial reports the number of ex-felons whose voting rights were restored as 156,000, and that 26,000 of those individuals had voted in November 2016. https://www.washingtonpost.com/opinions/virginias-breakthrough-on-rectifying-an-enormous-injustice/2017/06/11/c90e3808-4d52-11e7-9669-250d0b15f83b_story.html?utm_term=.b0528b5bfd05.

128. "Are Felons More Likely to Vote for Democrats over Republicans?" by ProCon.org, March 7, 2014. This website contains statements by Republicans and Democrats about the partisan implications of restoring ex-felon voting rights, including the 2004 statement by Marty Connor to the *Washington Post* that ex-felons are likely to support Democrats. http://felonvoting.procon.org/view.answers.php?questionID=000662.

129. "Florida: An Outlier in Denying Voting Rights," by Erkia Wood, The Brennan Center for Justice, December 16, 2016. This report has national and state-based statistics on felon disenfranchisement. "Florida is one of only three states with a lifetime voting ban for people with felony convictions. The strict law disenfranchises 1.6 million citizens, including 21 percent of the state's voting-age African Americans." https://www.brennancenter.org/publication/florida-outlier-denying-voting-rights.

Also see: "Florida's felons inch closer to regaining right to vote," by Dan Sweeney, *Sun-Sentinel*, December 31, 2016. Ten percent of Florida's voting age population can't vote because of criminal records. http://www.sun-sentinel.com/news/florida/fl-voting-rights-felons-20161231-story.html.

Also see: "Epic Fight Over Florida's Political Future Looms As Constitutional Amendment to Restore Felon Voting Rights Clears Hurdle," by Lulu Friesdat, AlterNet.org, April 27, 2017. This is an update on a prospective state ballot measure to amend the Florida

Constitution to restore felon voting. http://www.alternet.org/activism/
epic-fight-over-floridas-political-future-looms-constitutional-amend-
ment-restore-felon.

130. "No, 1.8 million dead people aren't going to vote in November," by
Phillip Bump, *The Washington Post*, October 18, 2016. This piece recounts
Trump's oft-recreated claims that more than 1 million dead people will be
voting—but not likely for him. The *Post*'s traces the source of that claim,
notes how Trump manipulates a nonissue into a fake threat, and shows
how dead people do not vote. The real-life challenge for election officials
is keeping their voters lists accurate after people die or move, in both
cases not being informed of the change. https://www.washingtonpost.
com/news/the-fix/wp/2016/10/18/no-1-8-million-dead-people-arent-
going-to-vote-in-november/?utm_term=.16e1f2247798.

Chapter 11: The Starting Line

131. "Jeff Sessions," wikipedia.org. Jeff Sessions' biography. https://en.wiki-
pedia.org/wiki/Jeff_Sessions.
See 103, for 1985 voter fraud prosecutions as US Attorney in Alabama:
"Why Republicans Can't Find the Big Voter Fraud Conspiracy: If the
last federal investigation is any guide, the answer is simple: It probably
doesn't exist," by Lisa Rab, *Politico Magazine*, April 2, 2017. See: "Names
of the American Civil War," wikipedia.org, for Confederate names
of American Civil War: https://en.wikipedia.org/wiki/Names_of_the_
American_Civil_War.

132. Same as 24: Democracy Diminished: State and Local Threats to Voting
Post-Shelby County, Alabama v. Holder, by NAACP Legal Defense Fund,
June 9, 2016.

133. Same as 81: "Alabama House Approves Redistricting Bill Over
Objections," by Kim Chandler, Associated Press, May 18, 2017.
Also see 66: "The State of Redistricting Litigation (March 2017 edition),"
by the Brennan Center For Justice.

134. "How the GOP Is Re-segregating the South: Republicans are using
the redistricting process to undermine minority voting power and
ensure their party's dominance," by Ari Berman, *The Nation*, February

20, 2012. This report describes GOP redistricting is an attempt to turn the GOP into a party of white voters in the South, while making Democrats a bastion of nonwhites. https://www.thenation.com/article/how-gop-resegregating-south/.

Also see: "Separate and Unequal Voting in Arizona and Kansas: Two states want to create a two-tiered voting system reminiscent of the Jim Crow South," by Ari Berman, *The Nation*, October 15, 2013. This report described how Arizona and Kansas "want to create a two-tiered voting system reminiscent of the Jim Crow South." https://www.thenation.com/article/separate-and-unequal-voting-arizona-and-kansas/.

135. Same as 108: "How Do Proof-of-Citizenship Laws Block Legitimate Voters?" by Stuart Naifeh, demos.org, August 25, 2014. This report summarizes the various state and federal laws and lawsuits surrounding the attempt to add documented proof of citizenship to the voter registration process.

Also see 24: Democracy Diminished: State and Local Threats to Voting Post-Shelby County, Alabama v. Holder, by NAACP Legal Defense Fund, June 9, 2016.

Also see: "Voter Identification, Proof of Citizenship for Voting and Provisional Ballots: A National Overview," by Wendy Underhill, National Conference of State Legislatures, August 25, 2016. This paper presented at NCSL's 2016 conference is an overview of proof of citizenship laws, including how Tennessee's law differs from Arizona, Kansas, Alabama, and Georgia. "The Tennessee approach is different than the Kansas approach because it only comes into play when there is reason to doubt citizenship, rather than creating a requirement for all voters to show proof of citizenship." http://www.legis.nd.gov/files/committees/64-2014%20appendices/17_5143_03000appendixf.pdf.

136. "Additional Data Could Help State and Local Elections Officials Maintain Accurate Voter Registration Lists," US Government Accountability Office, June 2005. The report notes there is no single federal citizenship database, which has not changed since then. See numbered pages 14–17. "Two types of standard sources of identification, such as a driver's license, state identification or social security numbers are not useful because neither are evidence of citizenship." http://www.gao.gov/new.items/d05478.pdf.

137. "Register to Vote and Confirm or Change Registration," USA.gov. This is the US government's webpage with voter registration basics and links to state deadlines and voter ID requirements. https://www.usa.gov/register-to-vote.

138. "Register To Vote In Your State by Using This Postcard Form and Guide," vote.gov. This is the federal voter registration form and accompanying state registration details. Under Kansas, it described the documented proof of citizenship requirements and filing deadlines. https://vote.gov/files/federal-voter-registration_1-25-16_english.pdf.

139. "Same-day voter registration," ballotpedia.org. This lists the states with same-day or Election Day registration. Thirteen states and Washington, DC, had this option for the 2016 election. Three more states have passed it but it had not taken effect. https://ballotpedia.org/Same-day_voter_registration.

140. "Voter Identification Requirements | Voter ID Laws," by Wendy Underhill, National Conference of State Legislatures, June 5, 2017. This 2017 summary of state voter ID requirements says seventeen states in 2017 require state-issued photo IDs. "A total of 34 states have laws requesting or requiring voters to show some form of identification at the polls. 32 of these voter identification laws are in force in 2017. West Virginia's law, signed on April 1, 2016, goes into effect in 2018 and Iowa's law, signed on May 5, 2017, will not be fully implemented until 2019 . . . The remaining 18 states use other methods to verify the identity of voters. Most frequently, other identifying information provided at the polling place, such as a signature, is checked against information on file." http://www.ncsl.org/research/elections-and-campaigns/voter-id.aspx#Details.

141. Mark Martin, Secretary of State, et al v. Freedom Kohls, Toylanda Smith, Joe Flakes and Barry Haas, Supreme Court of Arkansas, No. CV-14-462, October 15, 2014.
This Arkansas Supreme Court ruling threw out the state's 2013 voter ID law as an unconstitutional "additional qualification" for eligibility. https://posting.arktimes.com/media/pdf/voter_id_opinion.pdf.
Also see: "Arkansas governor signs bill to reinstate voter ID law," by Andrew Demillo, Associated Press, March 24, 2017. The state's Republican Governor, Asa Hutchinson, signed a new voter ID law in

early 2017 reinstating the requirement. http://www.pbs.org/newshour/rundown/arkansas-governor-signs-bill-reinstate-voter-id-law/.

142. "Kris Kobach," by wikipedia.org. This biography article cites Kansas Secretary of State's history, including anti-immigrant activism. https://en.wikipedia.org/wiki/Kris_Kobach.

Also see: "Advocate for Tough Voting Rules to Steer Trump's Elections Commission," by Michael Wines and Julie Bosman, *The New York Times*, May 14, 2017. This profile follows his appointment as vice-chair by Trump to his Advisory Commission on Election Integrity. https://www.nytimes.com/2017/05/14/us/kris-kobach-voter-fraud.html?r-ref=collection%2Fsectioncollection%2Fus&action=click&contentCollec-tion=us&region=rank&module=package&version=highlights&contentPlacement=6&pgtype=sectionfront&_r=0.

143. "Arizona Taxpayer and Citizen Protection, Proposition 200 (2004)," ballot-pedia.org. The text and litigation summary of Arizona's 2004 state ballot measure, Proposition 200. https://ballotpedia.org/Arizona_Taxpayer_and_Citizen_Protection,_Proposition_200_(2004).

Also see: "Uncovering Kris Kobach's Anti-Voting History," by Tomas Lopez and Jennifer L. Clark, The Brennan Center for Justice at New York University School of Law, May 11, 2017. https://www.brennancen-ter.org/blog/uncovering-kris-kobach%E2%80%99s-anti-voting-history.

144. Same as 142, "Kris Kobach," Wikipedia section on "Immigration lawsuits."

Also see: "The Man Behind Trump's Voter Fraud Obsession," by Ari Berman, *The New York Times* Magazine, June 18, 2017. This further details Kobach's anti-immigrant work. https://www.nytimes.com/2017/06/13/magazine/the-man-behind-trumps-voter-fraud-obsession.html?mcubz=2&_r=0.

145. Same as 134: "Separate and Unequal Voting in Arizona and Kansas: Two states want to create a two-tiered voting system reminiscent of the Jim Crow South," by Ari Berman, *The Nation*, October 15, 2013. This report recounts the efforts by Kansas and Arizona to add documented proof of citizenship to their state voter registration forms, notes how Arizona law blocked more than thirty thousand people from registering, notes its Kansas corollary stopped over seventeen thousand people from register-ing, and reports the 2013 US Supreme Court ruling against Arizona.

Also see: Arizona v. Inter Tribal Council of Arizona, Inc. (Amicus Brief), by the Brennan Center for Justice at New York University School of Law, June 17, 2013. This webpage summarized the Supreme Court case and has links to all the briefs filed by voting rights advocates. http://www.brennancenter.org/legal-work/arizona-v-inter-tribal-council-arizona-inc-amicus-brief.

146. Same as 103: "Why Republicans Can't Find the Big Voter Fraud Conspiracy: If the last federal investigation is any guide, the answer is simple: It probably doesn't exist," by Lisa Rab, *Politico Magazine*, April 2, 2017. This feature includes Kobach's 2010 comments on voter fraud burrowing into every corner of United States and illegal aliens voting in Kansas.

147. "Proof of US Citizenship for Voter Registration: NOTE: This requirement is effective January 1, 2013." GotVoterId.com. This is Kansas's website page describing its proof of citizenship requirement for voter registration. http://www.gotvoterid.com/proof-of-citizenship.html.
Also see: "Secretary of State Kris Kobach announces first conviction of noncitizen voting in Kansas," by Hunter Woodall, KansasCity.com, April 12, 2017. This report notes that Kobach is the nation's only secretary with power to prosecute voter fraud. http://www.kansascity.com/news/politics-government/article144256424.html.

148. "Appeals court nixes proof of citizenship for voting in Georgia," by Kristina Torres, *Atlanta Journal-Constitution*, September 11, 2016. This report recounts the history of the state's proof of citizenship laws for voter registration and efforts by Republicans to get the US Election Assistance Commission to include that requirement in its voter registration materials.http://www.ajc.com/news/state--regional-govt—politics/appeals-court-nixes-proof-citizenship-for-voting-georgia/wq0WTs7FtiqWe QQNHldaPP/.

149. Kobach et al. v. The United States Election Assistance Commission, by the Brennan Center for Justice at New York University School of Law, June 29, 2015. This webpage summarizes the 2015 suit by Arizona and Kansas against the US Election Assistance Commission over adding the requirement of citizenship to state voter registration forms. In 2013, the US Supreme Court overturned a 2004 Arizona law requiring citizenship proof for the federal voter registration

form. http://www.brennancenter.org/legal-work/kobach-et-al-v-united
-states-election-assistance-commission.

Also same as 144: "The Man Behind Trump's Voter Fraud Obsession," by
Ari Berman, *The New York Times* Magazine, June 18, 2017.

150. Same as 149. Kobach et al. v. The United States Election Assistance
Commission, by the Brennan Center for Justice at New York University
School of Law, June 29, 2015.

151. League of Women Voters v. Newby, by the Brennan Center for
Justice at New York University School of Law, June 1, 2017. This
page summarizes the litigation surrounding the unilateral decision by
US Election Assistance Commission executive director Brian Newby
to include proof of citizenship instructions from three states on the
EAC's federal voter registration materials. It also notes how prior academic research has found that 7 percent of voters could be disenfranchised by this requirement. https://www.brennancenter.org/legal-work/
league-women-voters-v-newby.

152. Same as 151. League of Women Voters v. Newby, by the Brennan Center
for Justice at New York University School of Law, June 1, 2017.

153. Same as 144: "The Man Behind Trump's Voter Fraud Obsession," by Ari
Berman, *The New York Times* Magazine, June 18, 2017.

154. "Kris Kobach supports Donald Trump's assertion millions voted illegally,"
by Tim Carpenter, *The Topeka Capital-Journal*, November 30, 2016. Kansas
Secretary of State Kris Kobach agrees with Trump that as many as 3 million noncitizens voted illegally. http://cjonline.com/news/2016-11-30/
kris-kobach-supports-donald-trump-s-assertion-millions-voted-illegally.

155. "Noncitizen Voting: The Missing Millions," by Christopher Famighetti,
Douglas Keith, Myrna Perez, by the Brennan Canter for Justice at New
York University School of Law, May 5, 2017. This report surveyed the
ten counties with the largest noncitizen populations in United States to
see the extent of noncitizen voting in 2016—following Trump's claims
that upwards of 3 million immigrant illegally voted, thus preventing
him from a national popular vote majority. The Brennan Center found
only thirty cases of noncitizen voting out of 23.5 million votes cast in
2016 from these counties. https://www.brennancenter.org/publication/
noncitizen-voting-missing-millions.

156. Same as 142: "Advocate for Tough Voting Rules to Steer Trump's

Elections Commission," by Michael Wines and Julie Bosman, *The New York Times*, May 14, 2017. This profile of Kris Kobach's career notes his anti-immigrant advocacy, exaggerated claims of noncitizen voting and voter fraud, and how his policies have disenfranchised thousands while only one noncitizen voter was found—only nine people were successfully prosecuted for voter fraud.

157. "Critics See Efforts by Counties and Towns to Purge Minority Voters From Rolls," by Michael Wines, *The New York Times*, July 31, 2016. This report recounts how in Sparta, Georgia, local Republicans deployed sheriff deputies to question the voting credentials of blacks in 2015 before a mayoral election. https://www.nytimes.com/2016/08/01/us/critics-see-efforts-to-purge-minorities-from-voter-rolls-in-new-elections-rules.html?mcubz=2&_r=0.

158. "New Georgia Project releases financial records, renews voter push," by Kristina Torres, *The Atlanta Journal-Constitution*, February 11, 2016. This report recounts how the New Georgia Project submitted forty-one thousand voter registrations before the 2014 November election that were not processed—denying those registrants the vote that fall. After Election Day, eighteen thousand of those registrants were added to voter rolls. http://www.myajc.com/news/state—regional-govt—politics/new-georgia-project-releases-financial-records-renews-voter-push/JoatzFC6XHZQ8GcACOsRN/.

159. "Quick Response Evaluation: Accuracy of the Help America Vote Verification Program Responses," June 22, 2009 memo from Inspector General Patrick P. O'Carroll Jr., Social Security Administration, memo to SSA Commissioner. This internal agency report notes how using the last four digits of Social Security numbers, verses the full nine-digit numbers, creates twice as many false positives. "Our comparison of the FY 2008 verification responses for HAVV [SSA's system] and three other verification programs used by the States and employers —SSNVS, E-Verify, and SSOLV—showed that HAVV had a significantly higher no-match response rate. The three verification systems were developed for different purposes and [they] use varying tolerances because they require the full nine-digit SSN for verification. HAVV, on the other hand, does not use these same tolerances because it requires use of the last four digits of the SSN as mandated by the legislation. The no-match response rate for

the three other programs ranged from 6 to 15 percent, whereas HAVV's no-match response rate was 31 percent. Therefore, HAVV's no-match response rate was about two to five times higher than the no-match response rate for the other three programs." https://oig.ssa.gov/sites/default/files/audit/full/html/A-03-09-29115_7.html.

160. Same as 136: "Additional Data Could Help State and Local Elections Officials Maintain Accurate Voter Registration Lists," US Government Accountability Office, June 2005. This report notes matching used by states to verify voter registrations is error prone. It cites a Wisconsin study of its motor vehicle database, saying, "The matching and validation of names are complex and made more so when considering aliases and name changes, as are matches such as 'Margie L. Smith' with 'Margaret Smith' according to a Wisconsin study. The study estimated that even a 1 percent error rate on a match validating names, driver license numbers, etc. could generate tens of thousands of bad matches."

161. "Georgia judge sides with state in 'missing' voters case," by Kristina Torres, *The Atlanta Journal-Constitution*, October 29, 2014. This report describes the electronic matching process used by county election offices to verify the identities of new voters under direction of the Georgia Secretary of State. In addition to "pinging" the state driver's license database and federal Social Security database, it also pings the state Department of Corrections, whose information is not up-to-date. http://www.myajc.com/news/state—regional-govt—politics/georgia-judge-sides-with-state-missing-voters-case/AkvPr6mP9FiMXglh5NUlHJ/.

162. Same as 161: "Georgia judge sides with state in 'missing' voters case," by Kristina Torres, *The Atlanta Journal-Constitution*, October 29, 2014.

163. "From a Contentious Election to a Stronger Democracy: Strengthening democracy is the key to all other reforms," by Miles Rapoport, *The American Prospect*, October 6, 2016. http://prospect.org/article/contentious-election-stronger-democracy.

164. "Voting Advocates Announce a Settlement of 'Exact Match' Lawsuit in Georgia: Minor Typos and Data Entry Errors will No Longer Deny Eligible Georgians the Right to Register and Vote," press release from Lawyers Committee for Civil Rights Under Law and

others, February 10, 2017. https://lawyerscommittee.org/press-release/
voting-advocates-announce-settlement-exact-match-lawsuit-georgia/.

165. Same as 62: *Issues Related to Registering Voters and Administering Elections*,
US Government Accountability Office, June 2016. This report describes
how The Interstate Crosscheck program works on page 30 in footnote
45. "Participating states agree to provide information such as full name
and date of birth for those registered as well as turnout data, to Interstate
Voter Registration Crosscheck program administrators in January following a general election. Using the information provided by member
states, the Interstate Voter Registration Crosscheck program then provides states with data on potential duplicate registrations and potential
double voters."

166. BRIEF OF FORMER ATTORNEYS OF THE CIVIL RIGHTS
DIVISION OF THE UNITED STATES DEPARTMENT OF JUSTICE
AS AMICI CURIAE IN SUPPORT OF PETITIONER, filed March 9,
2017, at the US Supreme Court. This brief filed by former Republican
appointees at the Justice Department under President George W. Bush
urges the Supreme Court to hear an appeal of a lower-court ruling that
found Ohio had illegally purged inactive voters under the National Voter
Registration Act of 1993. On pages 16–19, it describes the 2015 to 2016
activity of the Interstate Voter Registration Crosscheck Program, which
tries to identify possible duplicate registrations and combat double
voting. It notes that thirty states are participants, but only twenty-five
states used it as of February 2016. It reported that Georgia had 540,245
"potential voter registration duplications." In these states, including
Ohio, North Carolina, Michigan, Virginia, Nevada, and Colorado, more
than 5,935,000 voters were flagged as suspicious based on Crosscheck's
imprecise matching criteria. http://www.scotusblog.com/wp-content/
uploads/2017/03/16-980-cert-amicus-former-doj-attorneys.pdf.

167. BRIEF OF GEORGIA AND 14 OTHER STATES AS AMICI CURIAE
IN SUPPORT OF PETITIONER, filed March 10, at the US Supreme
Court. This is the brief filed by Georgia and fourteen other states urging
the Court to hear Ohio's appeal of a decision that found it had unconstitutionally purged 144,000 voters before the 2016 election. That ruling found the state did not follow the protocols in the National Voter
Registration Act of 1993. Georgia and other red states said the law was

ambiguous and they should be allowed to purge inactive voters. The Supreme Court will hear the case in its fall term. http://www.scotusblog.com/wp-content/uploads/2017/03/16-980-cert-amicus-Georgia.pdf.

CHAPTER 12: THE FINISH LINE

168. "Florida halts purge of noncitizens from voter rolls," by Steve Bousquet and Amy Sherman, *Tampa Bay Times*, March 27, 2014. Florida secretary of state stops a 2014 mass purge after local election officials revolted about his inaccurate voter purge lists. http://www.tampabay.com/news/politics/elections/florida-halts-purge-of-noncitizens-from-voter-rolls/2172206.

169. Same as 52: *The Fight to Vote*, by Michael Waldman, See pages 174–8 for Florida's massive 2000 voter purge.

170. "The National Voter Registration Act Of 1993 (NVRA): Questions and Answers," The United States Department of Justice. https://www.justice.gov/crt/national-voter-registration-act-1993-nvra.

171. Same as 129: "Florida: An Outlier in Denying Voting Rights," by Erika Wood, The Brennan Center for Justice at New York University School of Law, December 16, 2016.

172. Same as 52: *The Fight to Vote*, by Michael Waldman, See pages 174–8 for Florida'a massive 2000 voter purge.

173. "This Election Is Being Rigged—but Not by Democrats: The GOP's voter-suppression efforts are the real voter fraud," by Ari Berman, *The Nation*, October 17, 2016. This report cites of the results of a legal settlement in *NAACP v. Florida* where rerunning then secretary of state Katherine Harris's felon list with tighter criteria found twelve thousand voters were mistakenly purged in 2000. It also notes Trump's cry to "Stop Crooked Hillary From Rigging This Election," the crowd's "Lock her up" chants, and Trump's baseless accusations that Democrats steal millions of votes. https://www.thenation.com/article/this-election-is-being-rigged/.

174. Same as 168: "Florida halts purge of noncitizens from voter rolls," by Steve Bousquet and Amy Sherman, *Tampa Bay Times*, March 27, 2014.

175. "The GOP's Stealth War Against Voters: Will an anti-voter-fraud program designed by one of Trump's advisers deny tens of thousands their right to vote in November?" by Greg Palast, *Rolling Stone*, August

24, 2016. http://www.rollingstone.com/politics/features/the-gops-stealth-war-against-voters-w435890.

176. Same as 166: BRIEF OF FORMER ATTORNEYS OF THE CIVIL RIGHTS DIVISION OF THE UNITED STATES DEPARTMENT OF JUSTICE AS AMICI CURIAE IN SUPPORT OF PETITIONER, filed March 9, 2017, at the US Supreme Court. This brief was filed by six former Justice Department officials, including four who were appointed by George W. Bush and oversaw the DOJ's unsuccessful voter fraud prosecutions. They include: Colonel Karl S. "Butch" Bowers, Robert D. Popper, Bradley J. Schlozman, and Hans A. von Spakovsky. Pages 16–19 details the Interstate Voter Registration Crosscheck Program's 2016 activities, including twenty-five states' numbers of suspicious registrations totaling 5.9 million voters.

177. A Philip Randolph Institute, Northeast Ohio Coalition for the Homeless, Larry Harmon v. Jon Husted, Secretary of State, September 23, 2016 decision by the US Court of Appeals for the Sixth Circuit, File Name 16a0241p.06. This is the ruling that found Ohio had violated the National Voter Registration Act by purging inactive voters. The state appealed it to the US Supreme Court, which will hear it in its fall 2017 term. http://www.scotusblog.com/wp-content/uploads/2017/02/16-980-op-bel-6th-cir.pdf.

178. Same as 84: "The Supreme Court Could Make It Easier for States to Purge Voters: The Court has decided to hear a new case from Ohio, where Democrats were twice as likely as Republicans to be purged from the rolls in the state's largest counties," by Ari Berman, *The Nation*, May 30, 2017. This update on the Supreme Court agreeing to hear Ohio's appeal notes that the GOP-led purges were disproportionately in black and Democratic neighborhoods in its three largest cities: Cleveland, Columbus, and Cincinnati. "At least 144,000 voters in Ohio's three largest counties, home to Cleveland, Columbus, and Cincinnati, were purged since the 2012 election, with voters in Democratic-leaning neighborhoods twice as likely to be removed as those in Republican-leaning ones, according to a Reuters analysis. These cities are heavily Democratic, with large minority populations, and there was a clear partisan and racial disparity to the state's voter purge."

179. "Use it or lose it: Occasional Ohio voters may be shut out in November,"

by Andy Sullivan and Grant Smith, Reuters, June 2, 2016. The investigative report found the GOP secretary of state had disproportionately purged inactive voters in blue epicenters compared to nearby red regions. "In Cleveland's Cuyahoga County, 5 percent of voters in neighborhoods that backed Obama by more than 60 percent in 2012 were purged last year due to inactivity, according to the Reuters analysis of the voter lists. In neighborhoods where Obama got less than 40 percent of the vote, 2.5 percent of registered voters were removed for that reason. In Franklin County, home to the state capital Columbus, 11 percent of voters in Democratic-leaning neighborhoods have been purged since 2012 due to inactivity. Only 6 percent of voters in Republican-leaning neighborhoods have been purged. The disparity is especially stark in Hamilton County, where affluent Republican suburbs ring Cincinnati, which has one of the highest child-poverty rates in the country. In the heavily African-American neighborhoods near downtown, more than 10 percent of registered voters have been removed due to inactivity since 2012. In suburban Indian Hill, only 4 percent have been purged due to inactivity." http://www.reuters.com/article/us-usa-votingrights-ohio-insight-idUSKCN0YO19D.

180. Same as 84: "The Supreme Court Could Make It Easier for States to Purge Voters: The Court has decided to hear a new case from Ohio, where Democrats were twice as likely as Republicans to be purged from the rolls in the state's largest counties," by Ari Berman, *The Nation*, May 30, 2017. This report notes that 7,500 voters were put back on Ohio rolls after the Sixth Circuit ruled in September 2016.

181. "Upgrading Democracy: Improving America's Elections by Modernizing States' Voter Registration Systems," by *The Pew Center on The States/Election Initiatives*, November 2010. This is the report of Pew's Voter Registration Modernization Design Working Group. http://www.pewtrusts.org/~/media/legacy/uploadedfiles/pcs_assets/2010/upgradingdemocracyreportpdf.pdf.

182. "Who We Are," by EricStates.org/. About the Electronic Registration Information Center, which in 2016 had twenty states participating. http://ericstates.org/whoweare.

183. Same as 103: "Why Republicans Can't Find the Big Voter Fraud Conspiracy: If the last federal investigation is any guide, the answer is simple: It probably doesn't exist," by Lisa Rab, *Politico Magazine*, April

2, 2017. This report notes Trump incorrectly citing a Pew study at an October 2016 rally to make accusations of hordes of dead voters casting ballots. It includes responses by David Becker, who led Pew's Voter Registration Modernization Design Working Group and oversaw a series of studies and reports to make the case for better registration data systems.

184. "Sean Spicer wrongly uses Pew study to bolster claim that noncitizens vote in large numbers," by Lauren Carroll, politifact.com, January 25, 2017. This report notes Spicer's January 2017 comment mistakenly cites Pew's data to make false claims about noncitizen voting. http://www.politifact.com/truth-o-meter/statements/2017/jan/25/sean-spicer/sean-spicer-wrongly-uses-pew-study-bolster-claim-n/.

Also see: "Inaccurate, Costly, and Inefficient: Evidence That America's Voter Registration System Needs an Upgrade," by *The Pew Center on The States/Election Initiatives*, 2012. This is the Pew report that Spicer referenced: http://www.pewtrusts.org/~/media/legacy/uploadedfiles/pcs_assets/2012/pewupgradingvoterregistrationpdf.pdf.

185. "The Success of the Voter Fraud Myth," by The Editorial Board, *The New York Times*, September 20, 2016. This editorial contains the 2102 quote by Jim Greer on voter fraud being a marketing ploy. This editorial cited a *Washington Post*/ABC News poll on voter fraud where only 1 percent of respondents correctly answered how often it occurs. https://www.nytimes.com/2016/09/20/opinion/the-success-of-the-voter-fraud-myth.html?mcubz=2.

Also see: "Poll: Nearly half of Americans say voter fraud occurs often," by Emily Guskin and Scott Clement, *The Washington Post*, September 15, 2016. https://www.washingtonpost.com/news/the-fix/wp/2016/09/15/poll-nearly-half-of-americans-say-voter-fraud-occurs-often/?utm_term=.cd1ceb14af2b.

186. Same as 185: "The Success of the Voter Fraud Myth," by The Editorial Board, *The New York Times*, September 20, 2016.

187. "Ohio Voter Fraud Billboards Target Minorities," by Lauren Feeney, BillMoyers.com, October 11, 2012. This report described voter intimidation in three swing state cities with large black populations: "Billboards warning that voter fraud is a felony punishable with up to 3-and-a-half years and a $10,000 fine have been popping up in predominantly

black neighborhoods in Cleveland, Cincinnati, and Milwaukee. The ads are a blatant attempt at voter intimidation, say community leaders in Cleveland, where the signs were first noticed." http://billmoyers. com/2012/10/11/ohio-voter-fraud-billboards-target-minorities/.

188. "Voter Integrity Project boot camp teaches how to challenge voters," by Jane Porter and Billy Ball, IndyWeck.com, September 18, 2013. This report contains an interview with DeLancy where he said he could not be affiliated with the Republican Party and work the voter caging operations that his organization was doing. The report also says DeLancy took his inspiration from True The Vote. http://www.indyweek.com/indyweek/ voter-integrity-project-boot-camp-teaches-how-to-challenge-voters/ Content?oid=3721401.

189. "Judge: North Carolina counties must restore voters removed in 'insane' process," by Tribune News Services/Associated Press, November 4, 2016. This AP report recounts North Carolina restoring 6,700 voter registrations after a NAACP suit, where the "Voter Integrity Project" tried to purge thousands of voters. http://www.chicagotribune.com/news/ nationworld/ct-north-carolina-voter-purge-ruling-20161104-story.html.

190. North Carolina State Conference of the NAACP et al. v. North Carolina State Board of Elections et al, November 4, 2016 ruling by US District Court Judge Loretta C. Biggs ordering North Carolina counties to restore any voters purged within ninety days of the presidential election, noting that this violated the National Voter Registration Act of 1993. https://assets.documentcloud.org/documents/3214462/Order.pdf.

191. "Abbott signs voter ID, end of straight-party voting into law," by Chuck Lindell, *Austin American-Statesman*, June 1, 2017. This report notes how GOP Texas Gov. Greg Abbott signed into law a new slightly less restrictive voter ID bill and also eliminated the option of voting a straight party ticket starting in 2020. http://www.statesman.com/ news/abbott-signs-voter-end-straight-party-voting-into-law/5vb95W-3p0406a5mRgysEyL/.
Also see: "Redistricting," TexasTribune.org. This index of ongoing articles includes a May report that "Several Texas Republicans in Congress told the Tribune they want Gov. Greg Abbott to call a special session to redraw the state's congressional map. Yet a court filing from Texas

Attorney General Ken Paxton Thursday made clear Abbott isn't inter-
ested." https://www.texastribune.org/tribpedia/redistricting/.

192. North Carolina State Conference of the NAACP et al. v. Pat McCrory et
al. This is the July 29, 2016 ruling by the United States Court of Appeals
for the Fourth Circuit, No. 16–1468, written by Judge Diana Gribbon
Motz. The ruling struck down five anti-voter laws in North Carolina, saying they targeted black voters with "almost surgical" precision. https://
www.ca4.uscourts.gov/Opinions/Published/161468.P.pdf.

Also see: "Strict North Carolina Voter ID Law Thwarted After Supreme
Court Rejects Case," by Adam Liptak and Michael Wines, *The New
York Times*, May 15, 2017. This report notes the US Supreme Court
rejected the state's appeal of the Fourth Circuit's ruling, saying it
would like to rule on voting issues raised but the state's politics were
too messy to take the case. https://www.nytimes.com/2017/05/15/us/
politics/voter-id-laws-supreme-court-north-carolina.html?rref=collec-
tion%2Fbyline%2Fadam-liptak&action=click&contentCollection=unde-
fined&region=stream&module=stream_unit&version=latest&content-
Placement=2&pgtype=collection.

193. Same as 192: North Carolina State Conference of the NAACP et al. v.
Pat McCrory et al. This is the July 29, 2016 ruling by the United States
Court of Appeals for the Fourth Circuit, No. 16–1468, written by Judge
Diana Gribbon Motz.

194. "Some States Review Election Systems for Signs of Intrusion," by Emery
P. Dalesio and Geoff Mulvihill, Associated Press, June 8, 2017. The
report notes a Florida company, VR Systems, whose voter registration
database, which created precinct e-poll books in a handful of counties
in eight states, was hacked by Russia. The AP wrote, "North Carolina
state elections board director Kim Westbrook Strach said her office had
not been contacted by any federal officials about whether any of the 21
county election offices that use VR software were targeted. Still, her office
was contacting county boards about potential breaches. The news of a
reported Russian hacking attempt surprised Bill Brian, elections board
chairman in Durham County, which experienced problems with VR
Systems' electronic poll books on Election Day. The issue forced officials to abandon the system, issue paper ballots and extend voting hours,
but officials there said that trouble did not appear to have been caused

by hacking." https://www.apnews.com/2dfaa4ca0053447d868eeb0d-d4153c2a?utm_campaign=SocialFlow&utm_source=Twitter&utm_medium=AP_Politics.

195. "Top-Secret NSA Report Details Russian Hacking Effort Days Before 2016 Election," by Mathew Cole, Richard Esposito, Sam Biddle and Ryan Grimm, TheIntercept.com, June 5, 2017. The report presents a classified May 2017 National Security Agency document that recounts how Russia intelligence agencies targeted private contractors servicing voter registration systems before the 2016 election. It notes how in Durham County, North Carolina, e-poll books failed at precincts "causing chaos and long lines, which triggered election officials to switch to paper ballots and extend voting later into the evening." George McCue, BOE deputy director, said, "There was some investigation there, essentially no evidence came out of it indicating there was any problem with the product," he said. "It appears to be user errors at different points in the process, between the setup of the computers and the poll workers using them." https://theintercept.com/2017/06/05/top-secret-nsa-report-details-russian-hacking-effort-days-before-2016-election/.

CHAPTER 13: THE PLAYBOOK: DO EVERYTHING

196. "Donald Trump is wrong. Rigging an election is almost impossible: This is how hard it would be to pull off widespread voter fraud," by Ari Berman, *The Washington Post*, August 5, 2016. This report notes when Trump started raising voter-fraud claims in the campaign. https://www.washingtonpost.com/posteverything/wp/2016/08/05/donald-trump-is-wrong-rigging-an-election-is-almost-impossible/?utm_term=.053d77ddbd53.

197. "Republicans limit early voting in Marion County, letting it bloom in suburbs," by Fatima Hussein, IndyStar.com, August 10, 2017. Excerpt: "Most telling, Hamilton County saw a 63 percent increase in absentee voting from 2008 to 2016, while Marion County saw a 26 percent decline. Absentee ballots are used at early voting stations." http://www.indystar.com/story/news/2017/08/10/silencing-vote-data-shows-unequal-barrier-indiana-polls/435450001/.

198. "New Voting Restrictions in Place for the 2016 Election," by the Brennan

Center for Justice at New York University School of Law, November 2, 2016. This report notes new restrictions were in place in fourteen states, including: Alabama, Arizona, New Hampshire, Ohio, South Carolina, Texas, Virginia, and Wisconsin. https://www.brennancenter.org/sites/default/files/analysis/New_Restrictions_2016.pdf.

199. "Will North Carolina Lead the Way to a New South? Progressives like Reverend Barber and candidates like Deborah Ross are hoping to assemble a multiracial coalition to defeat a conservative backlash," by Joan Walsh, *The Nation*, November 7, 2016. This report notes black turnout in early voting had fallen by 16 percent because there were 158 fewer polling places in forty counties. https://www.thenation.com/article/will-north-carolina-lead-the-way-to-a-new-south/.

200. "NCGOP Sees Encouraging Early Voting, Obama/Clinton Coalition Tired, Fail to Resonate in North Carolina," North Carolina Republican Party, November 6, 2016. This press release said black voting was down and white voting was up, compared to 2012. http://us2.campaign-archive1.com/?u=f3100bc5464cbba2f472ddf2c&id=e4b9a8fb19.

201. Same as 192: North Carolina State Conference of the NAACP et al. v. Pat McCrory et al. This is the July 29, 2016 ruling by the United States Court of Appeals for the Fourth Circuit, No. 16–1468, written by Judge Diana Gribbon Motz, striking down North Carolina's omnibus anti-voter legislation following the US Supreme Court's 2013 gutting of the Voting Rights Act of 1965.

202. League of United Latin American Citizens v. Perry 548 US 399 (2006). This is the US District Court ruling cited by the Fourth Circuit opinion over North Carolina's 2013 anti-voter laws. The US Supreme Court affirmed the District Court's conclusions. https://supreme.justia.com/cases/federal/us/548/399/opinion.html.

203. Same as 192: North Carolina State Conference of the NAACP et al. v. Pat McCrory et al.

204. Same as 192: North Carolina State Conference of the NAACP et al. v. Pat McCrory et al. See footnote 7, page 47.

205. "Don Yelton, GOP Precinct Chair, Delivers Most Baldly Racist *Daily Show* Interview of All Time," by Joe Coscarelli, *New York* magazine, October 24, 2013. This is the article cited in the footnote in the Fourth Circuit's ruling against North Carolina with Don Yelton's statement on "lazy blacks"

and North Carolina's 2013 voter ID law. http://nymag.com/daily/intelli-gencer/2013/10/don-yelton-racist-daily-show-interview.html.

206. Same as 192: North Carolina State Conference of the NAACP et al. v. Pat McCrory et al. See footnote 7, page 47.

207. Same as 196: "Donald Trump is wrong. Rigging an election is almost impossible: This is how hard it would be to pull off widespread voter fraud," by Ari Berman, *The Washington Post*, August 5, 2016. The report quotes US District Judge James Peterson's Jury 2016 ruling that threw out Wisconsin's stricter voter ID law. "A preoccupation with mostly phantom election fraud leads to real incidents of disenfranchisement, which undermine rather than enhance confidence in elections."

208. "Texas Agrees to Soften Voter ID Law After Court Order," by Michael Wines, *The New York Times*, August 4, 2016. https://www.nytimes.com/2016/08/04/us/texas-agrees-to-soften-voter-id-law-after-court-order.html?mcubz=2&_r=0.

209. Same as 199: "Will North Carolina Lead the Way to a New South? Progressives like Reverend Barber and candidates like Deborah Ross are hoping to assemble a multiracial coalition to defeat a conservative backlash," by Joan Walsh, *The Nation*, November 7, 2016. This report cites the final 2016 campaign efforts by Democrats.

210. Same as 93: *The Deceit of Voter Fraud*, by Bob Hall and Isela Gutierrez, Democracy North Carolina, April 2017. This report goes into great detail how Gov. Pat McCrory's reelection campaign fabricated voter fraud charges against six hundred people in a failed attempt to overturn the results of his narrow loss in November 2016.

211. Ruthelle Frank, et al., v. Scott Walker, Case no. 11-CV-01128, League of United Latin American Citizens (LULAC) of Wisconsin, et al., v. Judge David Deininger, et al, Case no. 12-CV-00185, United States District Court Eastern District of Wisconsin, decision issued April 29, 2014. This ruling noted that Wisconsin's restrictive voter ID law prevented three hundred thousand people from voting. https://www.scribd.com/document/221004483/WiscVoterID-195-Decision.
Also see: "Texas, Wisconsin Photo ID Wins Could Help Nearly 1 Million Registered Voters," by the Brennan Center for Justice at New York University School of Law, October 10, 2014. http://www.brennancenter.org/press-release/texas-wisconsin-photo-id-wins-could-help-nearly-

1-million-registered-voters. But by 2016, Wisconsin had adopted a new voter ID law. See: "Voting Laws Roundup 2016," by the Brennan Center, April 18, 2016. http://www.brennancenter.org/analysis/voting-laws-roundup-2016.

212. Same as 13: *Shattered: Inside Hillary Clinton's Doomed Campaign*, by Jonathan Allen and Amie Parnes, Crown, 2016. http://www.penguinrandomhouse.com/books/247611/shattered-by-jonathan-allen-and-amie-parnes/9780553447088/ See pages 396–98.

SECTION III: THE RECOUNTS
CHAPTER 14: WHAT HAPPENED?

213. Same as 13: *Shattered: Inside Hillary Clinton's Doomed Campaign*, by Jonathan Allen and Amie Parnes, Crown, 2016. See pages 382–394.

214. Same as 1: "It's time to bust the myth: Most Trump voters were not working class," by Nicholas Carnes and Noam Lupu, *Washington Post*, June 5, 2017. Excerpt: "Among people who said they voted for Trump in the general election, 35 percent had household incomes under $50,000 per year (the figure was also 35 percent among non-Hispanic whites), almost exactly the percentage in NBC's March 2016 survey. Trump's voters weren't overwhelmingly poor. In the general election, like the primary, about two thirds of Trump supporters came from the better-off half of the economy."

215. "Elections: State Progress, Federal Train Wreck; State secretaries bask in smooth Election Day, joust in Washington's battles," by Miles Rapoport, *The American Prospect*, March 2, 2017. Rapoport is the former secretary of state in Connecticut, and president of both Dēmos and Common Cause. "The chaos and conflict at the polls that was feared by many did not materialize . . . Two issues, however, were too fraught with partisan conflict to achieve any consensus on the part of the assembled secretaries of state: Russian hacking and calculated interference in the election, and the president's claim of massive voter fraud." http://prospect.org/article/elections-state-progress-federal-train-wreck.

216. "Russian Cyber Hacks on US Electoral System Far Wider Than Previously Known," by Michael Riley and Jordan Robertson, Bloomberg.com, June 13, 2017. Excerpt: "Russia's cyberattack on the US electoral system before Donald Trump's election was far more widespread than has been publicly revealed, including incursions into voter databases and software systems in almost twice as many states as previously reported . . . In all, the Russian hackers hit systems in a total of 39 states, one of them said."https://www.bloomberg.com/news/articles/2017-06-13/russian-breach-of-39-states-threatens-future-u-s-elections.

217. "Exit Interview: Michigan Elections Director Christopher Thomas: Thomas looking forward to having time to actually think about elections,"

ElectionLine Weekly, June 29, 2017, http://www.electionline.org/index.php/2017/2233-electionlineweekly-june-29-2017.

218. "Donald Trump Warned Of A 'Rigged' Election, Was He Right?" by Jonathan D. Simon, *MintPress News*, January 24, 2017, https://www.mintpressnews.com/donald-trump-warned-of-a-rigged-election-was-he-right/224326/.

219. Same as 218: "Donald Trump Warned Of A 'Rigged' Election, Was He Right?" by Jonathan D. Simon, *MintPress News*, January 24, 2017.

220. "Hacking The Diebold Machine," YouTube.com, August 2, 2007. In 2006, Princeton University's Ed Felten testified before Congress and demonstrated the hack, saying it was possible to "silently transfer votes from one candidate to another," and that "launching it requires access to a single voting machine for as little as one minute." https://www.youtube.com/watch?v=HBqGzgxcfAk.

    For full hearing, with Barbara Simons testimony, see: "Electronic Voting Machines: Verification, Security, and Paper Trails," by Committee on House Administration, September 28, 2006, https://archive.org/details/gov.house.cha.2006.09.28.

221. "Feds believe Russians hacked Florida election-systems vendor," by Evan Perez, Shimon Prokupecz, and Wesley Bruer, CNN.com, October 10, 2016. http://www.cnn.com/2016/10/12/politics/florida-election-hack.

222. "Inside The Recount: Jill Stein and a ragtag team of computer experts decided to take America's elections to court. Here's how it all went wrong," by Steve Friess, NewRepublic.com, Feb. 15, 2017, https://newrepublic.com/article/140254/inside-story-trump-clinton-stein-presidential-election-recount.

223. Same as 222: "Inside The Recount: Jill Stein and a ragtag team of computer experts decided to take America's elections to court. Here's how it all went wrong," by Steve Friess, NewRepublic.com, Feb. 15, 2017.

224. "A Fair Election? Serious, Hard-to-Explain Questions Arise About Trump Vote Totals in 3 Key States: Voting rights advocates are scrambling to see if recounts are feasible in Wisconsin, Michigan and Pennsylvania," by Steven Rosenfeld, AlterNet.org, November 18, 2016, http://www.alternet.org/election-2016/fair-election-serious-hard-explain-questions-arise-about-trump-vote-totals-3-key.

225. Same as 222: "Inside The Recount: Jill Stein and a ragtag team of

computer experts decided to take America's elections to court. Here's how it all went wrong," by Steve Friess, NewRepublic.com, Feb. 15, 2017.

226. "Experts Urge Clinton Campaign to Challenge Election Results in 3 Swing States," by Gabriel Sherman, *New York* magazine, November 22, 2016, http://nymag.com/daily/intelligencer/2016/11/activists-urge-hillary-clinton-to-challenge-election-rcsults.html.

227. January 26, 2017, email from Jill Stein, HQ@Jill2016.com, summarizing the recount process and next steps on the eve of Trump's inauguration.

228. Same as 227: January 26, 2017 Email from Jill Stein.

CHAPTER 15: THE FINAL SWING STATES

229. "What We Know and Don't Know about Election 'Hacks' in 2016," by David Becker, Center for Election Innovation and Research, June 6, 2016, https://www.electioninnovation.org/news/2017/6/6/what-we-know-and-dont-know-about-election-hacks-in-2016.

230. "Ex-NSA head suggests US also hacks political parties," by Joe Uchill, *The Hill*, October 18, 2016, http://thehill.com/policy/cybersecurity/301667-former-cia-and-nsa-head-suggests-us-also-hacks-political-parties.

231. "Cyberwar for Sale: After a maker of surveillance software was hacked, its leaked documents shed light on a shadowy global industry that has turned email theft into a terrifying—and lucrative—political weapon." by Mattathias Schwartz, *The New York Times* Magazine, January 8, 2017. https://www.nytimes.com/2017/01/04/magazine/cyberwar-for-sale.html?_r=0.

232. "The GOP's cyber election hit squad," by Steven Rosenfeld, April 22, 2007, FreePress.org, http://freepress.org/article/gops-cyber-election-hit-squad.

233. "The Verifier - Polling Place Equipment - Current," by VerifiedVoting.org. This interactive page by Verified Voting allows viewers to zoom into states and see the voting machinery in every county in America. https://www.verifiedvoting.org/verifier/#.

234. Same as 227: January 26, 2017, email from Jill Stein.

235. "1.7 million people in 33 states and D.C. cast a ballot without voting in the presidential race," by Philip Bump, *Washington Post*, December 14, 2016, https://www.washingtonpost.com/news/the-fix/

wp/2016/12/14/1-7-million-people-in-33-states-and-dc-cast-a-ballot-without-voting-in-the-presidential-race/?utm_term=.ad146cd2a5db.

236. December 21, 2026, email from Jan BenDor, Michigan Election Reform Alliance's statewide coordinator, to author. "As we explained in our press conference on Monday [December 19], Michigan election officials sabotaged the Stein recount by lying about what the 1954 law actually says, and what the 1979 promulgated recount rules actually say." See: "Michigan Election Reform Alliance News Conference," by Walter Sorg, YouTube.com, December 20, 2016. https://www.youtube.com/watch?v=7qSmPymx9G0.

237. "Voter Suppression in the Mirror and Looking Forward: How much damage occurred in 2016, and what's in store for 2018 and beyond?" by Miles Rapoport, *The American Prospect*, August 7, 2017. http://prospect.org/article/voter-suppression-mirror-and-looking-forward.

238. "What 6 Top Election Experts Are Saying About the Next Big Step in the 2016 Recount," by Steven Rosenfeld, Alternet.org, November 29, 2016, http://www.alternet.org/election-2016/what-6-top-election-experts-are-saying-about-next-big-step-2016-recount.

239. "The Real Story of the Recount," by Bob Fitrakis, *Columbus Free Press*, January 4, 2017, http://columbusfreepress.com/article/real-story-recount.

240. "Don't Tread on My Vote," by Michelle Parker and Sharon Purvis, http://mzpiterations.com, July 2017. This website launches a campaign in Allegheny County to "push a referendum for the November 7, 2017, ballot that would enact an ordinance that creates a Voting Process Review Commission to evaluate Allegheny County's voting system." http://mzpiterations.com/.

241. December 23, 2016, letter from Jonathan S. Abady, lead attorney representing the Greens, to US Attorney General Loretta Lynch. https://d3n8a8pro7vhmx.cloudfront.net/jillstein/pages/27984/attachments/original/1482528938/FINAL_ECBA_letter_to_DOJ_re_election_investigation_(00270677x9CCC2).pdf?1482528938.

242. Same as 241: Letter from Jonathan S. Abady, see page 7.

243. Same as 239: "The Real Story of the Recount," by Bob Fitrakis, *Columbus Free Press*, January 4, 2017.

244. October 23, 2017, email from Justin Levitt, Professor of Law and Associate Dean for Research at Loyola Law School, Los Angeles, CA. See: "Federal

Prosecution of Election Offenses, Seventh Edition," Department of Justice, May 2007. This is the DOJ's 344-page manual for prosecutors in the Civil Rights Division's Voting Section. https://www.justice.gov/sites/default/files/criminal/legacy/2013/09/30/electbook-0507.pdf.

245. "On Tyranny: Lessons From The Twentieth Century," June 2017 lecture by Timothy Snyder at International Festival of Arts and Ideas, New Haven, Connecticut, posted on Youtube, June 17, 2017, https://www.youtube.com/watch?v=_4T9aGYoONU.

246. Same as 229: "What We Know and Don't Know about Election 'Hacks' in 2016," by David Becker, Center for Election Innovation and Research, June 6, 2016.

247. "Inside the Trump Bunker, With Days to Go: Win or lose, the Republican candidate and his inner circle have built a direct marketing operation that could power a TV network—or finish off the GOP," by Joshua Green and Sasha Issenberg, bloomberg.com, October 26, 2016, https://www.bloomberg.com/news/articles/2016-10-27/inside-the-trump-bunker-with-12-days-to-go.

248. "Information Operations and Facebook," by Jen Weedon, William Nuland and Alex Stamos, Facebook, Inc., April 27, 2017. See page 11, section entitled, "A Deeper Look: A Case Study of a Recent Election." https://fbnewsroomus.files.wordpress.com/2017/04/facebook-and-information-operations-v1.pdf.

249. "Connecting The Dots: Political Microtargeting and the Russia Investigation," by Kate Brannen, JustSecurity.org, May 18, 2017, https://www.justsecurity.org/41199/connecting-dots-political-microtargeting-russia-investigation-cambridge-analytica/ This report includes excerpts from an interview with Sen. Mark Warner, D-VA, the Senate Intelligence Committee vice-chair, where he said the committee was looking at whether Russians were targeting Clinton voters in swing states with fake news via their social media accounts.
Also see: "Who Hacked the Election? Ad Tech Did. Through 'Fake News,' Identity Resolution and Hyper-Personalization," by Jonathan Albright, Medium.com, July 30, 2017, https://medium.com/@d1gi/who-hacked-the-election-43d4019f705f.

250. Same as 245: "On Tyranny: Lessons From The Twentieth Century," June

2017 lecture by Timothy Snyder at International Festival of Arts and Ideas, New Haven, Connecticut, posted on Youtube, June 17, 2017.

251. Same as 230: "Ex-NSA head suggests US also hacks political parties," by Joe Uchill, *The Hill*, October 18, 2016.

252. "Were 2016 vote counts in Michigan and Wisconsin hacked? We double-checked," by Walter R. Mebane Jr. and Matthew Bernhard, June 6, 2017, https://www.washingtonpost.com/news/monkey-cage/wp/2017/06/06/were-2016-vote-counts-in-michigan-and-wisconsin-hacked-we-double-checked/?utm_term=.4e769fa2eb9e.

253. "Watch: Hackers Demonstrate How to Crack Into Electronic Voting Machine in Minutes: Disturbing footage from the DEF CON 25 hacker convention," by Lulu Friesdat, AlterNet.org, July 29, 2017, http://www.alternet.org/investigations/def-con-25-hackers-get-electronic-voting-machines-and-e-poll-books-minutes.

254. Same as 252: "Were 2016 vote counts in Michigan and Wisconsin hacked? We double-checked," by Walter R. Mebane Jr. and Matthew Bernhard, June 6, 2017.

255. Same as 237: "Voter Suppression in the Mirror and Looking Forward: How much damage occurred in 2016, and what's in store for 2018 and beyond?" by Miles Rapoport, *The American Prospect*, August 7, 2017.

256. "Wisconsin Strict ID Law Discouraged Voters, Study Finds," by Michael Wines, *New York Times*, September 25, 2017. https://www.nytimes.com/2017/09/25/us/wisconsin-voters.html.

CHAPTER 16: THE ELECTORAL COLLEGE

257. "Why I Will Not Cast My Electoral Vote for Donald Trump," by Christopher Suprun, *New York Times*, Dec. 6, 2016, https://www.nytimes.com/2016/12/05/opinion/why-i-will-not-cast-my-electoral-vote-for-donald-trump.html?mcubz=2&_r=0.

258. December 29, 2017, letter to Congressional Black Caucus by Ruby Sales and Ann Billingsley (www.spirithouseproject.org) and Ann Massaro (Women and Allies).

259. "At Least 50 Trump Electors Were Illegitimately Seated as Electoral College Members: More evidence surfaces as calls mount to challenge

congressional ratification of Electoral College vote," by Steven Rosenfeld, AlterNet.org, January 4, 2017, http://www.alternet.org/election-2016/least-50-trump-electors-were-illegitimately-seated-electoral-college-members.

260. COUNTING ELECTORAL VOTES—JOINT SESSION OF THE HOUSE AND SENATE HELD PURSUANT TO THE PROVISIONS OF SENATE CONCURRENT RESOLUTION 2, House of Representatives, January 6, 2017. This is the Congressional Record and transcript of the Electoral College ratification debate on January 6, 2017. https://www.congress.gov/congressional-record/2017/01/06/house-section/article/H185-8.

261. PERMISSION TO PLACE IN THE RECORD A STATEMENT REGARDING THE JOINT SESSION OF ELECTION, House of Representatives, January 6, 2017. These are the extended remarks by Rep. Shiela Jackson Lee, D-TX, filed in the Congressional Record. https://www.congress.gov/congressional-record/2017/01/06/house-section/article/H190-3.

AFTERWORD

262. "The Other Right-Wing Tidal Wave Sweeping America: Federal and State Preemption of Local Progressive Laws: Preemption allows corporations to boost their profits by suppressing local government power, community groups and citizens," by Don Hazen and Steven Rosenfeld, AlterNet.org, February 25, 2017, http://www.alternet.org/activism/other-right-wing-tidal-wave-sweeping-america-federal-and-state-preemption-local-progressive.

263. "Recidivism Watch: Trump's claim that millions of people voted illegally," by Glenn Kessler, *Washington Post*, January 24, 2017, https://www.washingtonpost.com/news/fact-checker/wp/2017/01/24/recidivism-watch-trumps-claim-that-3-5-million-people-voted-illegally-in-the-election/?utm_term=.bd3f388d4c36.

264. "Trump's voter fraud experts registered in 3 states," by Garance Burke, Associated Press, January 31, 2017, https://apnews.com/80497cfb5f05 4c9b8c9e0f8f5ca30a62.

265. "The Latest Voter Fraud Lie," by The Editorial Board, *The New York Times*, Feb. 13, 2017, https://www.nytimes.com/2017/02/13/opinion/the-latest-voter-fraud-lie.html?_r=0.

266. "Trump's Former Aide Concedes There Was No Voter Fraud In New Hampshire: Corey Lewandowski is not reading from the same script," by Sam Stein, *The Huffington Post*, February 20, 2017, http://www.huffingtonpost.com/entry/trump-voter-fraud-corey-lewandowski_us_58ab2331e4b07602ad56d2f4.

267. "Trump's voter fraud claims undermine the democratic process and his presidency," by Dan Balz, *The Washington Post*, January 25, 2017, https://www.washingtonpost.com/politics/trumps-voter-fraud-claims-undermine-the-voting-system-and-his-presidency/2017/01/24/a71d58ee-e288-11e6-a453-19ec4b3d09ba_story.html?utm_term=.2e1c1a730607.

268. Jeff Sessions, Wikipedia biography. Excerpt: "In 1985, Sessions prosecuted three African American community organizers in the Black Belt of Alabama, including Martin Luther King Jr.'s former aide Albert Turner, for voter fraud, alleging tampering with 14 absentee ballots. The prosecution stirred charges of selective prosecution of black voter registration. The defendants, known as the Marion Three, were acquitted of all charges by a jury after three hours of deliberation." https://en.wikipedia.org/wiki/Jeff_Sessions#U.S._Attorney.

269. "Trump administration confirms plans to drop key claim against Texas Voter ID: The US Department of Justice confirmed Monday it plans to ditch its longstanding position that Texas lawmakers purposefully discriminated against minority voters by passing the nation's strictest voter identification law in 2011," by Jim Malewitz, *The Texas Tribune*, Feb. 27, 2107, https://www.texastribune.org/2017/02/27/voter-id-case-trumps-team-drops-argument-against-texas/.

270. "Obama's DOJ Fought Texas Voter ID Law. Trump's New Civil Rights Chief Offered Tips On Writing It: That's not a great sign for voting rights," by Ryan Reilly, *The Huffington Post*, January 25, 2017, http://www.huffingtonpost.com/entry/civil-rights-division-trump-texas-voter-id_us_5887a75fe4b098c0bba6f72d.

271. "Restore lawful enforcement policies in the Civil Rights Division," March 28, 2017 letter to US Attorney General Jeff Sessions, from two-dozen Republicans including former George W. Bush administration

DOJ staffers. https://www.scribd.com/document/343306400/Letter-to-AG-Sessions-on-Civil-Rights-Division Also see: "A Department of Justice, But For Whom?" by Joshua Matz and Leah Litman, April 7, 2017, TakeCare.com, https://takecareblog.com/blog/a-department-of-justice-but-for-whom.

272. Same as 166: former Republican DOJ appointees' letter to Sessions. Also see: "The Justice Department's Voter Fraud Scandal: Lessons," by Adam Gitlin and Wendy Weiser, The Brennan Center for Justice at New York University Law School, January 6, 2017. https://www.brennancenter. org/publication/justice-departments-voter-fraud-scandal-lessons.

273. "Presidential Executive Order on the Establishment of Presidential Advisory Commission on Election Integrity," The White House, May 11, 2017, https://www.whitehouse.gov/the-press-office/2017/05/11/presidential-executive-order-establishment-presidential-advisory.

274. Same as 166: former Republican DOJ appointees' letter to Sessions.

275. June 28, 2017, letter from Kris Kobach, Vice-Chair, Presidential Commission on Election Integrity, to state election directors. https://twitter.com/vanitaguptaCR/status/880479649817649152.

276. Tweets by Michael McDonald, University of Florida US election turnout expert, on July 1, 2017. "Make no mistake, this is a cynical, calculated ploy engineered by Kobach who knew some states could never respond . . . So when Kobach says states are 'hiding' he knew in advance some states couldn't share data. His request set states up so he can accuse them." https://twitter.com/ElectProject/status/881139025440124928.

277. Tweet by Donald J. Trump, July 1, 2017, 6:07 AM. https://twitter.com/realDonaldTrump/status/881137079958241280.

278. "The Bogus Voter-Fraud Commission," by the Editorial Board, The New York Times, July 22, 2017, https://www.nytimes.com/2017/07/22/opinion/sunday/the-bogus-voter-fraud-commission.html?_r=0.

279. "Presidential Advisory Commission on Election Integrity, Mission, Procedures and Topics for Consideration," July 19, 2017, meeting, broadcast by C-SPAN.org, https://www.c-span.org/video/?431521–3/presidential-advisory-commission-election-integrity-mission-procedures-topics-consideration.

280. "President Trump Appoints Country's Worst Vote Suppressor to His 'Election Integrity' Commission," by Rick Hasen, Election Law Blog, June 29, 2017. http://electionlawblog.org/?p=93444.

281. June 28, 2017, letter from T. Christian Herren Jr., Chief, Voting Section, US Department of Justice, to state election directors to review "voter list maintenance procedures in each state." https://twitter.com/JessicaHuseman/status/880499901179809792.

282. Same as 272: "The Justice Department's Voter Fraud Scandal: Lessons," by Adam Gitlin and Wendy Weiser, The Brennan Center for Justice at New York University Law School, January 6, 2017.

283. Husted v. A. Philip Randolph Institute, Supreme Court of the United States blog. "Issue(s): Whether 52 U.S.C. § 20507 permits Ohio's list-maintenance process, which uses a registered voter's voter inactivity as a reason to send a confirmation notice to that voter under the National oter Registration Act of 1993 and the Help America Vote Act of 2002." http://www.scotusblog.com/case-files/cases/husted-v-philip-randolph-institute/.

284. "Justice Dept. sides with Ohio's purge of inactive voters in case headed to Supreme Court," by Sari Horwitz, The Washington Post, August 8, 2017. Excerpt: "The move is part of a broader campaign by the Trump administration to support restrictions on who is eligible to vote, a radical change in philosophy from the previous Justice Department, which sued a number of states over voting laws that it deemed discriminatory against minorities." "https://www.washingtonpost.com/world/national-security/justice-department-reverses-position-to-allow-ohio-to-purge-inactive-voters-from-rolls/2017/08/08/e93c5116-7c35-11e7-9d08-b79f191668ed_story.html?utm_term=.ce60184c4704.

285. Gill v. Whitford, Supreme Court of the United States blog. "Issue(s): (1) Whether the district court violated Vieth v. Jubelirer when it held that it had the authority to entertain a statewide challenge to Wisconsin's redistricting plan, instead of requiring a district-by-district analysis; (2) whether the district court violated Vieth when it held that Wisconsin's redistricting plan was an impermissible partisan gerrymander, even though it was undisputed that the plan complies with traditional redistricting principles; (3) whether the district court violated Vieth by adopting a watered-down version of the partisan-gerrymandering test employed by the plurality in Davis v. Bandemer; (4) whether the defendants are entitled, at a minimum, to present additional evidence showing that they would have prevailed under the district court's test, which the court announced only

after the record had closed; and (5) whether partisan-gerrymandering claims are justiciable." http://www.scotusblog.com/case-files/cases/gill-v-whitford/.

286. "Ratf**ked: The True Story behind The Secret Plan to Steal America's Democracy," by David Daley. Printing with post-2016 epilogue available at: https://www.amazon.com/gp/aw/d/1631493213/ref=mp_s_a _1_1?ie=UTF8&qid=1499989700&sr=8–1&pi=AC_SX236_SY340_ QL65&keywords=ratfuked&dpPl=1&dpID=41vTVqsxuXL&ref=plSrch #featureBulletsAndDetailBullets_secondary_view_div_1500080267818.

287. "Democrats Better Focus on the Races That Matter in '18 or We Will Have Another Decade of Right-Wing Extremists in Charge: Retaking the House in 2018 slows the GOP. Only governors can stop GOP gerry-manders and political monopolies through 2031," by Steven Rosenfeld, AlterNet.org, July 14, 2017, http://www.alternet.org/election-03918/democrats-who-dont-want-live-republican-extremists-another-de-cade-need-focus-2018.

288. Same as 262: "The Other Right-Wing Tidal Wave Sweeping America: Federal and State Preemption of Local Progressive Laws: Preemption allows corporations to boost their profits by suppressing local govern-ment power, community groups and citizens," by Don Hazen and Steven Rosenfeld, AlterNet.org, February 25, 2017.

289. "ALEC's Scary Plan For Electing Your Senators: The radical right is intent on destroying democracy as we know it," by David Daley, Alternet.org, July 22, 2017, http://www.alternet.org/alecs-scary-plan-electing-your-senators.

290. "We're Supposed to Be a Democracy, But Half the GOP Is OK with Postponing 2020's Election: A party full of delusions exposes the dark under-belly of America," by Steven Rosenfeld, AlterNet.org, August 10, 2017.

291. "Voting Machine Digital Ballot Images Could Let Public Recount Elections, But Many Locales Aren't Saving or Sharing This Data: Publicly verified elections are key to de-corrupting our democracy," by John Brakey, AlterNet, June 8, 2017, http://www.alternet.org/activism/voting-machine-digital-ballot-images-could-let-public-recount-elections.

292. "Citizen Scientists Comb Images To Find An 'Overexcited Planet,'" by Joe Palca, National Public Radio, June 1, 2017, http://www.npr.org /2017/06/01/530766624/citizen-scientists-comb-images-to-find-an-over-excited-planet.

INDEX

intimidation tactics, 78, 95–96, 120, 184–185n187

Iowa Caucuses, 2016 election, 4, 8–14, 27, 149n15

"The Iowa caucuses: An accident of history," 148–149n8

Iowa Democratic Party, 10–11

Iowa's nightmare revisited: Was correct winner called? (Jacobs), 149n15

Issenberg, Sasha, 121, 195n247

Issues Related to Registering Voters and Administering Elections, 158n62

Issues Related to State Voter Identification Laws, 158n61

"It's time to bust the myth: Most Trump voters were not working class," 147n1

J

Jackson, Simon, 46

Jacobs, Jennifer, 149n15

Jacobson, Jeff, 55–56

Jankowski, Chris, 42, 48–49

Jayapal, Pramila, 128

Jeff Sessions, wikipedia.org, 172n131, 198n268

Jefferson, David, 109

Jim Crow South, xxiv, 72, 96, 162, 172–173n134, 175n145

"Judge: North Carolina counties must restore voters removed in 'insane' process," 185n189

Judges Find Wisconsin Redistricting Unfairly Favored Republicans (Wines), 163n85

Justice Department Suing NYC Board Of Elections Over Last Year's Pre-Primary Mass Voter Purge (Tempey), 151n30

"Justice Dept. sides with Ohio's purge of inactive voters in case headed to Supreme Court" (Horwitz), 200n284

JustSecurity.org, "Connecting The Dots: Political Microtargeting and the Russia Investigation" (Brannen) May 18, 2017, 195n249

K

KansasCity.com, "Secretary of State Kris Kobach announces first conviction of noncitizen voting in Kansas" (Woodall) April 12, 2017, 176n147

Kaplan, Eric, 161n80

Kasdan, Diana, 167n110

Keith, Douglas, 177n155

Kemp, Brian, 78–82, 135–136

Kerry, John, xiii, 110, 115

Kessler, Glenn, 197n263

"Key Question for Supreme Court: Will It Let Gerrymanders Stand?" (Wines), 160n75

King, Martin Luther, Jr., 69, 132

Knight, John, 170n122

Kobach, Kris, 74–78, 82, 85–86, 91, 133–135, 138, 175n142, 199n275

Kobach et al. v. The United States Election Assistance Commission, 176–177n149

Kozikowski, Debra, 4–5

"Kris Kobach supports Donald Trump's assertion millions voted illegally" (Carpenter), 177n154

"Kris Kobach" wikipedia.org, 175n142

L

LaCapria, Kim, 150n22

Lachman, Samantha, 163–164n88

Lajevardi, Nazita, 62, 167n109

"The Latest Voter Fraud Lie" (The Editorial Board), 198n265

Lawrence Livermore National Library, 109

Court: Will It Let
Gerrymanders Stand?"
(Wines) April 21, 2017, 160n75
"The Latest Voter Fraud Lie" (The
Editorial Board) Feb. 13, 2017,
198n265
"Plaintiffs Claim Bias During
Closing Argument Against
Texas Voter ID Law"
(Fernandez) Sept. 22, 2014,
170n124
"Strict North Carolina Voter ID
Law Thwarted After Supreme
Court Rejects Case" (Liptak
and Wines) May 15, 2017,
186n192
"The Success of the Voter Fraud
Myth" (Editorial Board) Sept.
20, 2016, 184n185
"Texas Agrees to Soften Voter
ID Law After Court Order"
(Wines) Aug. 4, 2016, 189n208
"For Voting Rights Advocates,
Court Decision Is 'Temporary
Victory,'" (Wines) May
16,2017, 160–161n78
"When Does Political
Gerrymandering Cross a
Constitutional Line?" (Liptak)
May 15, 2017, 159n672
New York Times, 64
"Why I Will Not Cast My Electoral
Vote for Donald Trump"
(Suprun) Dec. 6, 2016, 196n257
"Wisconsin Strict ID Law
Discouraged Voters, Study
Finds" (Wines) Sept. 25, 2017,
196n256
The New Yorker, "Will Keith Ellison
Move the Democrats Left? By
running for the D.N.C. chair, the
Minnesota congressman hopes to

lead a populist opposition against
Trump" (Cunningham) Feb. 27
2017, 154n44
Newby, Brian, 76–78, 177n151
NewRepublic.com, "Inside The
Recount: Jill Stein and a ragtag
team of computer experts decided
to take America's elections to
court. Here's how it all went
wrong" (Friess) Feb. 15, 2017,
192n222
The News and Oberserver, "Will third
time be a charm for those who
want NC Supreme Court to invali-
date election maps?" (Blythe) May
30, 2017, 169–170n121
Ney, Bob, 54–57
Nichols, John, 155n51
Nielson, Lindsay, 167n109
"No, 1.8 million dead people aren't
going to vote in November"
(Bump), 172n130
No Party Preference (NPP), 25–26
noncitizen voting, 77, 165n94,
176n147, 177–178n156, 177n155,
184n184
"Noncitizen Voting: The Missing
Millions" (Famighetti, Keith,
Perez), 177n155
North Carolina Republican Party,
Nov. 6, 2016, 188n200
North Carolina, State Board of
Elections, April 2017, 53
*North Carolina State Conference of the
NAACP et al. v. North Carolina State
Board of Elections et al*, 185n190
*North Carolina State Conference of the
NAACP et al. v. Pat McCrory et al.*,
186n192
North Carolina voter discrepencies,
109
North Carolina voter hijacks, 96–97

Voter Integrity Project of North
   Carolina, 90–93
voter laws, 61–66, 168n117
voter machine hacking, 123, 192n220,
   192n221, 193n229, 193n230
voter purges, 22, 41–50, 83, 90–92, 124,
   135–136, 162–163n84, 180–181n167,
   180n166, 181–182n175, 181n168,
   181n173, 182–183n179, 185n189
voter registration database problems,
   22–23, 173n136, 174n137, 174n138,
   184n184, 186–187n192
voter registration laws, 71–78
Voter Registration Modernization
   Design Working Group, 88
voter registration verification,
   178–179n159, 178n158, 178n159,
   179–180n164, 179n161
voter suppression, 30, 132–133, 135,
   167n109, 199n280
"Voter Suppression in the Mirror
   and Looking Forward: How
   much damage occurred in 2016,
   and what's in store for 2018 and
   beyond?" (Rapoport), 194n237
"Voter Suppression Works"
   (McElwee), 167n108
"Voter Turnout in Presidential
   Elections: 1828–2012" (American
   Presidency Project), 165n95
votes, intentions of nation's founders,
   35
"Voting Advocates Announce a
   Settlement of 'Exact Match'
   Lawsuit in Georgia: Minor Typos
   and Data Entry Errors will No
   Longer Deny Eligible Georgians
   the Right to Register and Vote,"
   179–180n164
"Voting Law Changes: Election
   Update" (Weiser and Kasden),
   167n110

voting laws, 167n110
voting laws, restrictive, 164n90
"Voting Laws Roundup 2013"
   (Brennen Center for Justice),
   168n117
"Voting Laws Roundup 2017"
   (Brennan Law Review), 165n96
"Voting Machine Digital Ballot
   Images Could Let Public
   Recount Elections, But Many
   Locales Aren't Saving or Sharing
   This Data: Publicly verified elections are key to de-corrupting our
   democracy" (Brakey), 201n291
voting machine tampering, 19–20,
   108–110, 141, 196n253
voting machines, xxi–xxii
voting machines, assumptions of
   integrity, 113
voting maching verification, 201n291
voting operating rules, gaming,
   35–39
voting rights, 58–59, 61–67,
   171–172n129
Voting Rights Act, 1965 (VRA), 20,
   31, 43–44, 47, 64–66, 92, 96, 120,
   127–128, 133, 168n115
"The Voting Rights Act of 1965" (US
   Department of Justice), 167n111
"For Voting Rights Advocates, Court
   Decision Is 'Temporary Victory,'"
   (Wines), 160–161n78
Voting Section, US Department
   of Justice, letter, June 28, 2017,
   200n281
voting vigilantes, 90–93
VR Systems hack, 110

W
Waldman, Michael, 36, 58, 84–85,
   155n52
Walker, Scott, 118